I Prophesy To
Your Spiritual Womb
Two Nations Are
In Your Womb
Destined To Birth
Nations Into The Kingdom
- Ministry &
- Business(es)

Apostle Deborah
9-2017

APOSTOLIC *Women* BIRTHING NATIONS!

"A 21ST CENTURY GUIDE FOR 21ST CENTURY MINISTRY"

BY: APOSTLE DEBORAH L. ANDERSON

"AND THE SEED OF THE WOMAN SHALL CRUSH THE HEAD OF THE ENEMY"
GEN. 3:15

APOSTOLIC WOMEN BIRTHING NATIONS!
A 21ST CENTURY GUIDE FOR 21ST CENTURY MINISTRY
By Apostle Deborah L. Anderson

Edited by
Sheryl Norton, Patricia Moses, Elaine Donaldson

Published by
Fully Persuaded! Ministries International
Printed in the USA.

For bookings or orders
Contact Apostle Deborah L. Anderson
Fully Persuaded! Ministries International
P. O. Box 842114
Houston, Texas 77284-2114
Phone: 1-877-251-0077

Cover Design by
Jennifer Carrington of jcarrington+associates
Website http://www.jennifercarrington.com/

Author's Photographs by
Dayna Castelberg, Remember When...Photography, Katy, TX
www.rememberwhenphoto.photoreflect.com
Phone: 832-643-7500

ISBN: 978-0-9852285-6-9

Apostolic Women Birthing Nations!

A 21ST CENTURY GUIDE FOR 21ST CENTURY MINISTRY

Table of Contents

Table of Contents - continued

Dedication

I dedicate this book to my Heavenly Father, the Almighty God for saving my life as a testimony of His miraculous power of how He saved me and raised me from the dead.
To know and understand what Jesus meant by saying,
"No man takes my life from me, I lay it down,
because I have the power to take it up again."
John 10:18

To The Inheritance and Legacy of Generations of The Anderson Family birthed in prayer:

- To my late great, great grandfather, ***Pa Dan*** - A preacher, from whose seed I came forth who prayed that all of his generations be saved.
- To my mother, ***Lenora M. Anderson*** - Who taught me from a child how to pray. You always built my confidence and faith in God. You believed in me, telling me that I could do anything, for with God all things are possible.
- To my late father, ***Dennis Murphy Anderson*** - Thank you for teaching me the principle of sowing and reaping. By the beautiful garden you planted every year with fertile rich soil that you drove out to the country to haul back to use, your efforts brought the greatest crops, feeding us that which you had planted.
- To my father's sisters, my late ***Aunt Ronnie B. Bland*** and ***Aunt Aretha Powell*** - Who taught me the importance of

serving the Lord, who anointed our heads with oil, and prayed us through at the altar of Emanuel Temple COGIC. From a child you taught me the Holy Scriptures.

- To my only son, ***Rashon LaVelle Anderson*** - Who by his wisdom, love and honor, dismantled my fears and pushed me to purpose to birth my dreams and visions.
- To my brothers and sisters, ***Dorothy, Barbara, Patricia, Denise, Lawanna, Andrew Dennis, and Daryl*** - Who obliged me in all of my "great ideas" whether they thought it would work or not, and just simply agreed and said, *"Yeah Deb, you can do it!"* -Love you always, The Middle Child!
- To my nephew, the late ***Anthony D. Anderson***, and his wife ***Delorce*** - A pillar in our family and community, regarded as one of the greatest thinkers of our time, you always engaged us in intellectual and theological debates regarding life, family, education and religion. You kept us laughing and kept us in love towards each other. I miss you so much.
- To my first nephew, ***Andre Anderson*** - For your prophetic flow through your gift of poetry which blessed our family to understand the value of relational role play!

Dedication - continued

This book is also dedicated to all the generals, ambassadors, pioneers, forerunners, spiritual mothers, fathers, mentors and trailblazers of the five-fold ministry who have paved the way to bring many sons into the Kingdom for such a time as this.

- *Bishop Marie Pines, Apostle Patricia Holley and Bishop Eunice Groves, Pastor Audrine Scales* for being loving, nurturing, firm spiritual mothers in Zion who gracefully treated me as a daughter and groomed me for this work.
- *Dr. Cassandra Scott,* Pastor of Turning Point Faith Ministries whose 6 a.m. Prayer Line "breathed" life into me to speak again. You appointed me as a Director of the Tribe of Issachar and enabled me to speak again to release the sound of my Apostolic and Prophetic voice to rise up again. To all of the intercessors on the Tribe of Issachar who resuscitated me by supporting, trusting and following my leadership; to all of the spiritual mothers and the Directors of Cassandra Scott Ministries 6 a.m. Prayer Lines and their twelve Tribes of Israel.
- *Bishop Victor Akoh* (Nigeria), *Bishop John Carter* (Lagos), *Bishop Chris Obi* (S.A.) International Council of Bishops for the network to touch nations through your leadership and support of Fully Persuaded! Ministries.
- *Pastors Ed and Saundra Elaine Montgomery*, Abundant Life Cathedral under whose ministry I was born again and discipled during the Charismatic Movement in the 80's

under a ministry that was the first to pioneer the new things of God throughout all the churches in the region. Thank you Pastor Saundra for the grace for me to become a U-Win Leader, and teaching us by your elegance and grace how to be leading ladies.

- *Pastors Remus and Mia Wright and Pastor Del Jackson* under whose leadership and ministerial training I was first mentored and preached my first sermon leaving a legacy of being the first woman to ever preach at SPO Baptist Church 20 years ago! My service under your leadership was my apostolic training to learn the inner-workings of church administration, how to lay the foundation to build ministries, teaching and demonstrating prayer, praise, worship, and building a church for spiritual and numerical growth. Thank you for cultivating the seed - allowing me the opportunity to exercise my gifts by teaching the bible study series, "What Happens When Women Pray." I will never forget the impact and seeds sown to birth intercessory prayer.
- *Pastor Audrine Scales*, New Believers Word of Faith Ministries, my first mentor and friend, *Pastors Lang* and *Joan Mason* my first Assistant Pastors of Fully Persuaded Ministries, and all of my covenant ministry partners, who have labored in prayer, fasting, giving, endured hardness as good soldiers the sake of the Gospel of Jesus Christ. I commend you for the battle scars I have learned through you to wear as a Decorated General in the Lord's Army perfecting me for the work of Fully Persuaded! Ministries International. God Bless You.

Endorsements

It is with great pleasure that I endorse Apostle Deborah L. Anderson as a great and mighty apostolic woman of God in the twenty-first century. The calling of God upon her life is a call to the Nations. We welcome her to South Africa as a Kingdom Ambassador to the nation of South Africa.

Apostle Chris Obi
Potters Touch ministries
Newcastle, South Africa

To Honor a Woman who so deserves it! I give praise to God for Apostle Deborah Anderson, one of My Spiritual Daughters. I know the Lord gave her to me when He said to talk with her. From the first time we spoke I knew the Lord had something in store for us, and He has blessed our relationship ever since. We have talked for hours about the Lord, and she is obedient to Him beyond her humble submission to authority. I know she loves the Lord and takes care of His sheep. She is very intelligent and gives God all the glory for her talents and abilities. That's what I love about her. Beautiful, gifted and anointed, she is not big headed. Her love for people at times comes before her own needs. Apostle Anderson has a vision and with God on her side, all men will know it is the Lord's doing. Amen! So with all my love and congratulations, Your Spiritual Mother.

Apostle Patricia M. Holley
Glassboro NJ

I first met Apostle Deborah Anderson more than 10 years ago. It was obvious from the beginning that she was mantled for an apostolic assignment to move God's vision from abstract to reality, from shadow to substance, and to awaken a bold fresh awareness in every NATION to their Kingdom rights. Truly I stand with this Apostolic Prophetic voice (Isaiah 30:21) who has inbreathed the Kingdom for this 21st Century and is Enlightened, Equipped and Empowered prophetically and scholastically for this generation.

Bishop Marie Pines
Malkut Banah Global Fellowship
Galveston, TX

Apostle Deborah serves as the Coordinator/Representative of the APETAP MINISTERIAL ASSOCIATION United States of America Ambassador. I have endorsed and recognized her Apostleship and recommend her to all leaders ranging from apostle in the body. She is a woman of God. We are in support of you in Nigeria. The power of the highest is on you; fear not. Look up to Jesus - the author and finisher! All He said to you, He will make it good! Fear not; I see your adversaries bowing down to lick the dust of your feet. You are the best in creation! Don't allow your past and present to distract you from your future. God has something great for you! I see you taking over regions and territories. Honour shall be your portion. I see greater open doors for you this season!

Apostle Victor Akoh
Apostolic Ambassador & Priest to All Nations
APETAP Ministerial Alliance Association
Port Harcourt Nigeria

This book, ***Apostolic Women Birthing Nations!*** is a must read for those who desire to fulfill their call to the nations. Even though it is written to women who are 21st-century apostles and the like, it is a working tool for 21st-century ministry. It is a wonderful guideline also for men who are apostolic and touching the earth realm because God has called us as a people to cover the earth with the Gospel. I commend you my sister who has stepped out to pull this wonderful writing. I would even call it a thesis to touch those who need to understand this reformation that God has called us into this hour.

Bishop Walter E. Holmes
C.E.O. WEH Ministries
Leading Apostle of Apostolic & Prophetic Network
Senior Leader of Word of Faith CC

Apostle Deborah L. Anderson, today, I salute you for the work you have done to promote the kingdom through sharing your ability to lead others effectively, and now to present your versatile skills as an author. God sees you as a: A STRONG COURAGEOUS WOMAN – Able to walk around your "Jericho Walls" knowing they will fall. A DETERMINED TO SUCCEED WOMAN – Never allowing disappointments to become stumbling blocks. A FULLY PERSUADED WOMAN – Unstoppable in your pursuit for truth. A PIONEERING WOMAN – Determined to explore unchartered territory in order to provide a road map for others. A SENSITIVE WOMAN – One who is sympathetic to others needs and offering your talents and gifts to assist others in their success. A GIVING

WOMAN – Always seeking ways to enlighten, empower, and embrace others who are called to kingdom advancement. A FAVORED WOMAN – To know your worth and not seeking to flaunt it or be prideful about it is likened to one who knows that her Heavenly Father has graciously bestowed favor on her with Him and with men. The beauty of true covenant is when God is the author and the anchor that holds the parent and the child. Daughter soar as an eagle, rise to the highest mountain and survey what God has given you allowing Him to be the wind beneath your wings.

Apostle Eunice O. Groves,
Grace & Mercy Kingdom Fellowship
International Apostolic & Prophetic Connection
Grand Prairie, TX

FULLY PERSUADED
Ministries

For This Cause!

For this cause I Paul (Deborah), the prisoner of Jesus Christ for you Gentiles, If ye have heard of the dispensation of the grace of God which is given me to you-ward: How that by revelation he made known unto me the mystery; (as I wrote afore in few words, Whereby, when ye read, ye may understand my knowledge in the mystery of Christ) Which in other ages was not made known unto the sons of men, as it is now revealed unto his holy Apostles and Prophets by the Spirit;

That the Gentiles should be fellow heirs, and of the same body, and partakers of his promise in Christ by the gospel: Whereof I was made a minister, according to the gift of the grace of God given unto me by the effectual working of his power. Unto me, who am less than the least of all saints, is this grace given, that I should preach among the Gentiles the unsearchable riches of Christ; And to make all men see what is the fellowship of the mystery, which from the beginning of the world hath been hid in God, who created all things by Jesus Christ:

To the intent that now unto the principalities and powers in heavenly places might be known by the church the manifold wisdom of God, According to the eternal purpose which he purposed in Christ Jesus our Lord: In whom we have boldness and access with confidence by the faith of him. Wherefore I desire that ye faint not at my tribulations for you, which is your glory.

For this cause I bow my knees unto the Father of our Lord Jesus Christ, Of whom the whole family in heaven and earth is named, That he would grant you, according to the riches of his glory, to be strengthened with might by his Spirit in the inner man; That Christ may dwell in your hearts by faith; that ye, being rooted and grounded in love, May be able to comprehend with all saints what is the breadth, and length, and depth, and height; And to know the love of Christ, which passeth knowledge, that ye might be filled with all the fullness of God.

"Now unto him that is able to do exceeding abundantly above all that we ask or think, according to the power that worketh in us, Unto him be glory in the church by Christ Jesus throughout all ages, world without end"

Amen!

FULLY PERSUADED
Ministries

Author's Abstract

This book could not be written within the normal literary guidelines for one to be considered a prolific and professional writer. I admit that there may be instances where my writing may not be grammatically nor politically correct, but it will be spiritually accurate. Therefore, I am compelled and Fully Persuaded to write under the leading of the Holy Spirit the words of Jesus Christ that supports the revelatory writing style of this work to accomplish God's original intent that "the seed of the woman will crush the head of the enemy" (Genesis 3:15). It is written to empower and inspire the emerging new wineskins who are carrying an Apostolic and Prophetic anointing to advance the Kingdom in this time of reformation! It is intended to break strongholds of mis-conception (emphasis intended) of scriptures pertaining to church membership, and setting of beliefs imposed mainly through the use of systematic theology. Man's attempt to explain God through certain traditional religious dogma, and systematic theological methods have failed miserably. For this cause and time in the 21st Century, Church foundations, structures and Governmental systems have been experiencing Birth Pangs that have challenged the core foundations of Christian faith and the U.S. Constitution. This reformation requires a careful re-examination and re-evaluation of church membership, and the role women play in God's full plan of redemption, and the urgency of God's Kingdom Ambassadors to walk in their God ordained authority to impact nations with present truth.

Further, we intend to silence the argumentative debates against men and women who are called to minister and properly express the gifts of the Holy Spirit as prescribed in I Corinthians 12, Ephesians 4 and the full restoration of the foundational gifts of the Apostle and Prophet who have emerged and are sent in our time to "rebuild the old waste places, to be a repairer of the breach, and a restorer of paths to dwell in (Isaiah 58:12, KJV). This emerging 21st Century body of believers in Jesus Christ, who understand the Power of His Resurrection, will destroy the heretical false teaching mimicking the operation of the five-fold ministry gifts who are teaching that "it's not about a title." With infallible scriptural proofs to "back it up" we will speak into the valley of dry bones and stand upon the mountain of religion that "it is not about a title – but it is all about the FUNCTION of the ministry gifts of the Holy Spirit given to the Body of Christ (Ephesians 4:11). For the record we will show the significance of two vital functions of the Body that must be restored to full capacity in the 21st Century for 21st Century ministry - the Apostle and the Prophet. It is also written in defense of women who are called to walk in the Office as Apostles and Prophets. Beyond the persistent argumentative debates against women "to keep silent in the church" (I Corinthians 14:34, KJV), it addresses the more critical and relevant need for all Believers to re-examine and rediscover the purpose for their calling and the truth concerning their salvation. This book speaks to the subculture of those who have legislatively opposed and challenged foundational Christian beliefs, the inerrancy of The Holy Bible Scriptures, devalued, mocked and criticized the powerful anointing of the Holy Ghost and the dominion power given to the Ministers of God, and ignore the supremacy of the King of Kings who is the Head and the Chief Cornerstone of the "Building." The stone which the builders rejected is become the head of the corner: This is the Lord's doing, and it is marvelous in our eyes (Mark 2:10-11, KJV).

For the men who will embrace the SHIFT from church to kingdom and who will be brave, open-minded and respectful enough to honor the spiritual mothers, wives and women in their families who have helped to build their relationship and faith in God, giving birth to their dreams and visions through intercession, shut-ins, and prayers, do not let "the title" of this book harden your heart nor turn your back to hear what the Lord is saying. To all those men and women who has ever testified "my mother, my grandmother prayed for me" who read this book, it is my prayer that you will gain a better understanding of the role of the "help mete" God took from rib out of the side of the man to complete His creation, for dual dominion, fruitfulness and multiplication. Nations will understand the "Sonship" God established in both male and female in the garden of our Genesis (beginning).

In conclusion, while at first I did not want the title to give the impression that this book was written to be a defense for women, it is necessary to exalt the full governing authority of the Lordship of Christ over religious persuasion to prepare His Body to receive the Bride of Christ without spot or wrinkle. By paralleling the power of the seed with the duty and responsibility of the male to protect, love honor and cherish, to keep the garden and to defend, protect and nurture the seed of the woman, it is critical that we realize that it is the seed that is destined TO CRUSH THE HEAD OF THE ENEMY - all foreign and domestic! The voice of the Lord is walking again 'in the cool of the Garden of His creation' and calling once again to His creation against the voice of the enemy, "Adam, where are you?"

JESUS CHRIST, THE AUTHOR AND FINISHER OF OUR FAITH

Delivered and Presented By:

Apostle Deborah L. Anderson
Ambassador and Speaker of the House

Part One

THE BIRTH PANGS OF REFORMATION

Chapter 1:

RELEASE THE SOUND OF THE KINGDOM

"Until the Ancient of days came, and judgment was given to the saints of the most High; and the time came that the saints possessed the kingdom."
Daniel 7:22

Reformation is the process of reforming an institution or practice. For those who have been "in church all of your life," there is an awakening of the Spirit of God with a sound that is shaking nations and subduing kingdoms! The Sound of the Kingdom is abrupt and does not care what you have been accustomed to hearing or what you think you already know about God. It is a sound like our Emergency Broadcasting System ("EBS") that will interrupt your "regularly scheduled church program" to bring you a Message from the King of Kings and the Lord of Lords. It is a sound that will set the captives free from every stronghold that had you bound all of your life. It is apostolic and it is Prophetic and will shatter all unbelief, bringing into captivity every thought to the obedience of Christ (I Corinthians 10:13). Frankly, for those who have already been SHIFTED, there is a building of anticipation for a Kingdom movement of God to happen in our time that will take us into higher dimensions, greater realms of His glory, and deeper levels of worship, adoration and praise. We anticipate His arrival, His anointing to fill this place, to pierce the nation with the sound of the trumpet! So we blow the trumpet in Zion!

In the last days, no apologies can be given by those who preach the Gospel for violating the rules of "systematic theology" in order to break the barriers of institutionalized thinking that have confined the revelation of truth and the "unchained" preaching of the Gospel of the Kingdom. For "Unto you it is given to know the mystery of the kingdom of God: but unto them that are without, all these things are done in parables that by seeing they may see, and not perceive; and hearing they may hear, and not understand; lest at any time they should be converted, and their sins should be forgiven them (Mark 4:12). Truth when presented confronts mindsets that tears down strongholds and sets captives free of religious and spiritual bondage. For many strongholds upheld by the religious spirit that has gripped nations and suppressed the preaching of the Gospel of Kingdom, this book will be "a hard saying" as Jesus described aforetime in John 6:60-69, KJV:

"Many therefore of his disciples, when they had heard this, said,
'This is an hard saying; who can hear it?'
When Jesus knew in himself that his disciples murmured at it, He said unto them, Doth this offend you? What and if ye shall see the Son of man ascend up where He was before? It is the spirit that quickeneth; the flesh profiteth nothing: the words that I speak unto you, they are spirit, and they are life. But there are some of you that believe not. For Jesus knew from the beginning who they were that believed not, and who should betray him. And He said, Therefore

said I unto you, that no man can come unto me, except it were given unto him of my Father."

There is a subculture within the Church and in Governmental positions of leadership who profess to know Him yet will deny Him and the Apostles who are still speaking today. It will come as a hard saying for those who believe and teach others that the Office of the Apostle was done away with. You are in for a rude awakening! Apostolic and Prophetic ministries confront these strongholds and pull down such evil imaginations that have been systematically imposed upon the nations. Many cannot and will not hear THE SOUND of the Kingdom (John 6:60) because their ears have become dull of hearing by the years of denominationalism and whose hearts have become hardened to the truth by the spirit of offense. That's apostolic – THE VOICE of the Apostles offended religious and political rulers then and now in a time of one of the greatest reformations in the 21st Century.

"Wherefore also it is contained in the scripture, Behold, I lay in Zion a chief corner stone, elect, precious: and he that believeth on him shall not be confounded. Unto you therefore which believe he is precious: but unto them which be disobedient, the stone which the builders disallowed, the same is made the head of the corner, And a stone of stumbling, and a rock of offence, even to them which stumble at the word, being disobedient: whereunto also they were appointed."
I Peter 2:6-8

Further, in our Genesis, a very important mandate was given by God when Adam sinned and caused sin to come into the world, knowing both good and evil. The curse between the seed of the enemy and the seed of the woman created "enmity" by ruling powers since that day. The head of the enemy is a mindset, a set of false beliefs that have impacted every sphere of government that impacts and influences the shape and form our world. Religion especially has held the Body of Christ captive from manifesting the working of mighty miracles with signs and wonders like unto those who followed the ministry of the Apostles in the New Testament. We have witnessed so many leaders' prideful slip into the trap of religious and political systems to mask the gospel of the Kingdom, making the Word of God dull and of none effect. Consequently, a great war in heaven between what we believe is truth and right and what we believe is good and evil. Two voices spoke in the garden: the voice of God and the voice of satan. The voice of the serpent in the garden was once subtle at suggesting that what God said was not true. Conversely, the serpent is not subtle today and has boldly declared God's Word is not true on the issues of marriage. Political powers have endorsed the voice of the serpent and given the people through their "Voting Rights" the right to choose where there is no choice.

One of the greatest causes of the failure of religion to discern and uphold the truth is the masking by human ingenuity to "appear" as truth and light so that the whole world walks in deception. Thus, the boldness of apostolic preaching is an imperative apostolic mandate to "turn cities upside down" by the preaching of the Gospel of the Kingdom. There can be no compromise but to be valiant for the truth to deliver and birth nations to know their God and do exploits in the Kingdom. I have chosen to expose the darkness in order to bring the truth and the light of the naked and unashamed – unchained!

"Oh that I had in the wilderness a lodging place of wayfaring men; that I might leave my people, and go from them! For they be all adulterers, an assembly of treacherous men. And they bend their tongues like their bow for lies: but they are not valiant for the truth upon the earth; for they proceed from evil to evil,
And they know not me, saith the LORD!
Take ye heed every one of his neighbour, and trust ye not in any brother: for every brother will utterly supplant, and every neighbour will walk with slanders. And they will deceive every one his neighbour, and will not speak the truth: they have taught their tongue to speak lies, and weary themselves to commit iniquity.
Thine habitation is in the midst of deceit; through deceit they refuse to know me, saith the LORD"
Jeremiah 9:3-6

There comes a time when you must face your own fears and recognize as ministers of the gospel you have been entrusted with something so great that you cannot play small by shrinking back. With the great salvation that Christ has wrought for us to be free from the opinions of men, we should be more compelled and inspired than ever as Believers in the 21st Century to pick up the mantles of those forerunners, pioneers, trailblazers and generals of the past like Barbara Jordan, Sojourner Truth, Albert Einstein, Nelson Mandela, Dr. Martin Luther King, Jr., Martin Luther, John Alexander Dowie, and so many others that we may finish our course with joy. Just imagine the power of one voice like the Apostle Peter who seeing through the darkness over the sea dared to step out of the boat to be a miraculous change agent. He stepped out of something to walk into something being led by THE VOICE of one whose outstretched arm, and holy hand gave him the victory (Psalms 44:3)! Defying the natural to do something supernatural by a voice that said, "Come" and that voice is still speaking today! I feel the wind of the Holy Ghost PUSHING me to defy the natural to birth a nation! Mary the Mother of Jesus said to His disciples, "Whatever HE SAYS DO – DO IT!" And the water turned into wine! God is calling for the New Wineskins to COME!

The courage to write this book was inspired by one of my favorite quotes spoken by Nelson Mandela, who in 1994 became the first President of South Africa elected in a fully-representative democratic election. Mandela's inauguration brought together the largest number of Heads of State since the funeral of U.S. President John F. Kennedy in 1963. He birthed a nation with the idea of freedom from the oppression of apartheid because he heard the cry of men and women in travail.

"Our deepest fear is not that we are inadequate. Our deepest fear is that we are powerful beyond measure. It is our light, not our darkness, that most frightens us. Your playing small does not serve the world. There is nothing enlightened about shrinking so that other people won't feel insecure around you. We are all meant to shine as children do. It's not just in some of us; it is in everyone. And as we let our own lights shine, we unconsciously give other people permission to do the same. As we are liberated from our own fear, our presence automatically liberates others."
(Nelson Mandela)

WHOSE CRY DO YOU HEAR?

Is it the cry of the abuse of religious leaders that has crossed all denominational and racial lines leaving a nation wondering if there are any "real" people on the planet that know and are submitted to the cause of Jesus Christ? Is it the cry of thousands of men and women locked behind prison bars by a system that has a broad range in the disparity of sentencing and the pain of their mothers who cried out for help to the lawyers but received ineffective assistance of legal counsel, yet they got paid thousands of dollars and their children are in prison under mandatory minimums? Do you hear the cry of a nation whose soul is bleeding over the senseless murders of the children at Sandy Hook ELEMENTARY school, Columbine, Lone Star College in the State of Texas and around the nation who demand no ban on assault weapons because "they" have a right to bear arms and want to go hunting? Perhaps you hear the cry and the call to move beyond the four walls of "the building" and church programs to be an apostolic pioneer to blaze a path and be a repairer of the breach and a restorer of paths to dwell in?... I'm just saying.

Great movements have always been inspired by great voices of the past that brought change to nations by the power of one voice. Great governmental leaders have emerged to reform national policies to meet the demands of today, and great preachers have emerged to carry the mantles that lay dormant by great reformers and spiritual leaders with a new anointing of the Gifts of the Holy Spirit to birth nations. While I know that as an Apostle just like Paul and Peter the Apostolic and Prophetic voices will experience much opposition in the 21st Century because the "systems" fear change, especially the religious systems because of the abundance of revelation that is being given through Apostolic and Prophetic ministry gifts that inspire change and resistance by the status quo who want to "have church" as usual.

"For this cause I Paul, the prisoner of Jesus Christ for you Gentiles, If ye have heard of the dispensation of the grace of God which is given me to you-ward: How that by revelation he made known unto me the mystery; (as I wrote afore in few words, Whereby, when ye read, ye may understand my knowledge in the mystery of Christ. Which in other ages was not made known unto the sons of men, as it is now REVEALED unto his holy Apostles and Prophets by the Spirit; That the Gentiles should be fellow heirs, and of the same body, and partakers of his promise in Christ by the gospel."
Ephesians 3:1-6

There is now an abundance of revelation and understanding of all of the sciences connected to the seven spheres of society: business, government, education, arts, media and entertainment, family, and religion. Leaders of these spheres have influence and power over the nations. Many are stepping "out of the box and out of the boat" against the fear of theological and governmental systems to birth a nation into levels of spiritual freedom necessary to meet the needs for ministry in the 21st Century. In the 1960s when the nation demanded change from oppression and racism during the Civil Rights Movement, Dr. Martin Luther King, as the curtain was about to close on his life, prophetically spoke these words:

"Well, I don't know what will happen now. We've got some difficult days ahead. But it doesn't matter with me now, because I've been to the mountaintop. And I don't mind. Like anybody, I would like to live a long life. Longevity has its place. But I'm not concerned about that now. I just want to do God's will. And He's allowed me to go up to the mountain. And I've looked over. And I've seen the promised land. I may not get there with you. But I want you to know tonight, that we, as a people, will get to the promised land. And I'm happy, tonight. I'm not worried about anything. I'm not fearing any man. Mine eyes have seen the glory of the coming of the Lord."
(Dr. Martin Luther King)

Dr. King's Prophetic declaration still rings throughout the consciousness of our nation. Inspiration from the voices of great preachers and greater reformers of the past with a great cloud of witnesses are waiting for the manifestation of the Sons of God in the 21st Century to answer the cry of a nation. With the same bold confident assurance of his calling as a drum major for justice to march at moment in time that would not only free a nation, but birth a nation. Apostolic and Prophetic men and women hear THE SOUND and now answer the calling for the preaching of the Gospel of the Kingdom in the 21st Century.

A TIME OF REVELATION AND INCREASED KNOWLEDGE

To one of the minor prophets of the Old Testament God reveals how and to whom He lets in on His secrets of what He is going to do. A secret is only shared with those who can be trusted to hold in confidence some things that are going to be revealed at a certain time to others, "For surely the Lord will do nothing except he reveals it first to his servants the Prophets" (Amos 3:9). Whenever God begins to deal with the foundation of nations, systems, and generations He reveals these secret things to His servants the Prophets. The Prophet "sees" what God is saying and the Apostle is sent forth to also see and carry out the instructions. Revelation and increased knowledge in the 21st Century is necessary to establish the blueprint, the pattern for others to follow that will bless a nation or prepare for the judgment of a nation. The revelation of God is always a message given to Apostles and Prophets to pray, to warn, to see, to speak, to decree and to declare a

SHIFT to make every crooked place straight and correct everything God reveals that is out of order into divine order.

When God speaks to His Apostles and Prophets He sends His Word into a place of famine when His will is to bring economic and spiritual increase or revival to a city, a region, or a nation. These two foundational ministry gifts are not itinerant preachers who market themselves for an "engagement" with a motive of making money, their burning desire and passion is to deliver the message that God has revealed to them in secret to shout it from the rooftops. A true Apostle or Prophet's motive is the heart of God and not an evil intent to harm but to edify build up, encourage and strengthen based on the revelation and knowledge received from God's desire to do His will.

The Prophet Isaiah understood the time, his assignment, and knowledge of the purpose and the will of God and moved boldly in his season declaring, *"The Spirit of the Lord GOD is upon me; because the LORD hath anointed me to preach good tidings unto the meek; he hath sent me to bind up the brokenhearted, to proclaim liberty to the captives, and the opening of the prison to them that are bound" (Isaiah 61:1, KJV).* Ministry in the 21st Century is more difficult now but the anointing for boldness carried through the Issachar Factor is the anointing necessary to do the greater works that Jesus promised. There is a Prophetic unveiling of the mysteries of the Second Coming of Christ being revealed and boldly being released through great Apostolic and Prophetic voices manifesting the Sons of God. This unveiling of the mysteries of Christ is what the enemy has always been terrified that the nations will hear and understand as the fulfillment of the curse he received in the Garden of Eden is set to take place - the battle between the seed of satan and the seed of the woman that will crush the head of the enemy.

The head represents seats of power and thrones upon which we are seated in heavenly places "far above principalities and powers." The head also represents the seat of power and authority. It governs, dictates, legislates, rules and regulates its authority and maintains the control over nations. It exercises its powers and gives rights to the people of a nation. One of the most empowering (good) yet destructive (evil) seats of power is religion that dictates and governs how we know and interpret Scripture. To the big brother, this Kingdom movement is not another civil rights movement or violent uprising as you may suppose. *This is that which was prophesied by the Prophet Joel, that in the last days I will pour out my spirit upon all flesh, your old men shall dream dreams and your young men shall see visions and also upon my handmaidens will I pour out in those days of my Spirit, and they shall prophesy! (Acts 2:16-18 KJV)*

PROPHETIC PRONOUNCEMENT: TELL ALL MY DAUGHTERS TO PROPHESY!

APOSTOLIC AUTHORITY

Paul defends our authority as an Apostle by stating that his authority was not conferred upon him by man's hands, nor did he have to sit under scrutiny and observation on a pew for so many years, be licensed after years of matriculation in a theological seminary, preach his first sermon nor was he ordained in any ceremonial fashion. He is saying also that his commissioning was not based upon gender or any prescribed denominational preference. Paul says, *"Whereof I was made a minister, according to the gift of the grace of God given unto me by the effectual working of his power" (Ephesians 3:7, KJV).* That's apostolic – that's the important qualification for ministers of the Gospel to do what HE called you to do in this 21st Century. Now, to unruffle the feathers of religious spirits who are trembling right now, and for those on their way to the ceremony, it's okay! In fact I was licensed, ordained a minister and confirmed to the Office of Apostle with the full ceremonial regalia. However, we should understand that when God calls us to the ministry that the ceremony will be met by a fanfare of banners of praise and appreciation, but the true test of the calling will cause those who once praised and embraced you to turn the lights out and walk away from you!

INCREASED INTERPRETATION BY REVELATION

"How that by revelation he made known unto me the mystery; (as I wrote afore in few words, Whereby, when ye read, ye may understand my knowledge in the mystery of Christ) Which in other ages was not

made known unto the sons of men, as it is now revealed unto his holy Apostles and Prophets by the Spirit" (Ephesians 3:3, KJV)

The Gift of Revelation is being given in abundance upon His ministers which is the supernatural ability to function with signs and wonders and see the miraculous power of God. Revelation and interpretation causes the enemy of our soul to buffet us, more so now than ever before. How many people have you talked to over the course of the last six years especially have told you, or you have shared with them, that it seems like things are getting worse and worse? Some of the things we used to be able to handle, are getting more and more difficult to handle now. We thought the Columbine school shooting was bad, but the shooting of children at Sandy Hook made it worse. It is an Ephesians 3 time in history for the foundational gifts of the Spirit – The Apostle and The Prophet to bring the revelation of Christ and His Kingdom into the 21st Century. Revelation moves you forward while religion holds you back or keeps you stuck in the past. Religious teaching by any form of systematic devices to explain God by the wisdom of man will and has failed miserably.

With each new generation there is an increase in revelation, wisdom, knowledge and understanding ("But thou, O Daniel, shut up the words, and seal the book, even to the time of the end: many shall run to and fro, and knowledge shall be increased," Daniel 12:4). Apostolic ministry was birthed through the New Testament Church to carry out the same plan to birth a nation is not confined within an institutional or denominational structure. There is a stark contrast between Apostolic and Prophetic preaching that interprets scripture in Prophetic illumination by revelation that speaks to time and builds a foundation for truth in teaching of Christ that the mysteries of Christ that were not known in previous generations are being made known in our time.

For example, Paul's thorn in the flesh remains a mystery to men who interpret scripture without divine revelation. Paul writes,

"And lest I should be exalted above measure through the abundance of the revelations, there was given to me a thorn in the flesh, the messenger of Satan to buffet me, lest I should be exalted above measure"
II Corinthians 12:7

Many preachers have preached this text with a short-sighted conclusion that God did not want Paul to become too proud or boastful because of the revelation of Jesus Christ and the Gospel, that he would become what we call "big-headed" and that God had to somehow cripple Paul to keep him humble. Well, that is not what the text says is the complete interpretation of the reason of Paul's thorn in the flesh. The correct interpretation, which the "boastful" theologians who study hermeneutics (the art of biblical interpretation) have failed miserably in their use of this method to preach such a conclusion - requires a contextual analysis of the verses before and after it. The scripture before tells us, *"For though I would desire to boast, I shall not be a fool; for I will say the truth: but now I forbear, lest any man should think of me above that which he sees me to be, or that he hears of me" (II Corinthians 12:6).*

Without divine revelation there can be no application. The Apostolic Fathers were students of the Apostles where the principle of prophecy fulfillment was used as a divine approach to Bible interpretation. The interpretation and revelation then of this scripture which is more readily illuminated and apparent is that a messenger of Satan was sent to buffet Paul – ***"because of the abundance of the revelations"*** that was given to him! Truth confronts mindsets that have been passed on from one to another. Looking at the origin of hermeneutics, one would be cautious when using this method of bible interpretation:

> *The folk etymology places the origin (Greek: hermeneutike) with Hermes, the mythological Greek deity whose role is that of messenger of the Gods. Besides being mediator between the gods themselves, and between the gods and humanity, he leads souls to the underworld upon death. He is also considered the inventor of language and speech, an interpreter, a liar, a thief and a trickster. These multiple roles make Hermes an ideal representative figure for*

> *hermeneutics. As Socrates notes, words have the power to reveal or conceal, thus promoting the message in an ambiguous way. The Greek view of language as consisting of signs that could lead to truth or falsehood is the very essence of Hermes, who is said to relish the uneasiness of the recipients.*
>
> *Early use of hermeneutics places it within the boundaries of the sacred. The divine message can only be understood on its own terms, received with implicit uncertainty regarding its truth or falsehood. This ambiguity of message is an irrationality, a sort of madness inflicted upon the receiver. Only one who possesses a rational method of interpretation—an early hermeneutic—could define the truth or falsehood (thus the sanity) of a statement. (Wikipedia).*

The Apostles style of teaching and preaching always upset religious rulers then and upsets many today. Revelation moves you forward while religion holds you back or keeps you stuck in the past. Apostle John Eckhardt in his book, ***The Ministry Anointing of the Apostle,*** explains that "the teachings of men always benefit those in leadership positions. To no surprise, religious leaders often fight apostolic ministry the most. Religious leaders usually desire to keep the system intact, because it benefits them. They often resist change and fight Reformation" (Crusaders Ministries). Religious teaching by any form of systematic devices to explain God by the wisdom of man will and has failed miserably. Many are teaching, texting, and blogging night and day to convince people that there are no more apostles today, and that the gift was "done away with" after the first twelve were killed. They wish that were the case.

What really displeases the religious rulers about the style of these new wineskins is that Apostolic and Prophetic ministries do not "stick to the text" but preach, praise, prophesy and allow the Spirit of the Lord to freely move "unchained" by the letter of the Word. "Not that we are sufficient of ourselves to think anything as of ourselves; but our sufficiency is of God; Who also hath made us able ministers of the new testament; not of the letter, but of the spirit: for the letter killeth, but the spirit giveth life" (II Corinthians 3:5-6, KJV). The letter of the Word which according to the traditional mindset that is not acceptable and one is frowned upon as being unlearned and absolutely mad. Paul in his defense to King Agrippa was met with such religious hostility, "And as he thus spake for himself, Festus said with a loud voice, Paul, thou art beside thyself; much learning doth make thee mad" (Acts 26:14, KJV). This is a hard saying but if you're still reading, don't stop now.

STATE OF THE NATION

There is a Second Coming of Christ that is being birthed in the womb carried by the seed of the woman with the same purpose as was in His first coming: "To crush the head of the enemy." The nation has fallen into a greater moral and spiritual decline than at any other time in history. Pornography, sex, suicide as a solution to end human pain, divorce amongst pastors, same sex marriage, rebellion, murder, earthquakes, wars and rumors of wars, disobedient children, spirit of poverty "designed" so that the rich will get richer and the poor will get poorer – all of these are signs of fulfillment of end-time biblical prophecies. I expect that you are already seeing these prophecies being fulfilled in the 21st Century and therefore I answer the critical opinions of those who deny these birth pangs and those who have lost hope of the Second Coming of Christ:

"Knowing this first, that there shall come in the last days scoffers, walking after their own lusts, and saying, where is the promise of His coming? For since the fathers fell asleep,
All things continue as they were from the beginning of the creation."
2 Peter 3:3-4, KJV

PROPHETIC PRONOUNCEMENT: GET READY FOR THE KINGDOM!

In those days came John the Baptist, preaching in the wilderness of Judaea, And saying,

REPENT! FOR THE KINGDOM OF HEAVEN IS AT HAND
For this is he that was spoken of by the Prophet Esaias, saying,
The voice of one crying in the wilderness,
Prepare ye the way of the Lord, make his paths straight."
Matthew 3:1-3

Chapter 2:

GOD'S APOSTOLIC MANDATE OF WOMEN: TO CRUSH THE ENEMY'S HEAD

"And the LORD God said unto the serpent, Because thou hast done this, thou art cursed above all cattle, and above every beast of the field; upon thy belly shalt thou go, and dust shalt thou eat all the days of thy life: And
I WILL PUT ENMITY BETWEEN THEE AND THE WOMAN,
and between thy seed and her seed;
it shall bruise thy head,
and thou shalt bruise his heel"
Genesis 3:14-15(KJV)

ACCEPTING THE CALL

Your acceptance of the call to the work of the ministry will be made to God before you confess to your Pastor and profess your calling before the congregation. I grew up believing women were not called to preach because it was enforced by the religious thinkers of my time. It was talked about at family and group settings how sin came into the world because of Eve. How women were cursed because Eve ate the apple. After hearing it said so often within family groups, community circles and over the pulpit, I grew up believing that women were a curse to the world. Everything bad happening was caused because of a woman. Watching third world countries and the disgraceful positions of women and how they were being treated and seeing the head coverings and dresses from their neck to their feet because it was a shame for women to even be seen in public had an effect upon my confidence and covered me with shame to even announce that God had called me to preach!

Growing up at Pilgrim Baptist Church I had never seen or heard a woman preach, except on television through Katherine Kuhlman. All I saw was women praying, women giving the announcements, women teaching Sunday School classes. It was the women from our church's missionary board who gathered from house to house having missionary union meetings. My mother was a part of the Missionary Society and sometimes hosted their meetings at our house. I felt it a privilege and honor to help her get the house and desserts ready to serve them when they came. The women would come with a mission on what they were going to do to remodel rooms in the church, paint the walls, and what they were going to pray about that night. I watched them strategically implement strategies on ways they could do outreach and evangelism.

On some Friday nights, my uncles and aunts from my father's side of the family who were ministers and prayer warriors at Emmanuel Temple C.O.G.I.C. would come to our house to hold prayer meetings. Everybody in the family had to cancel everything they were doing to be in the prayer meeting.

It did not matter what you were doing in the house, if you were outside you had to come in. It was like an emergency drill at our house on Friday nights. The women would come wearing their long white dresses with collars up to the neck and the men had on black suits and ties. They would make a circle around us as we came into the living room. I have a sister who is a year younger than me and we could not look at each other in the circle because we would burst out laughing! The saints did not think anything was funny at that time and they would pray harder as we laughed harder.

But something happened after a while when they began to anoint our heads with oil. And they didn't say a dab will do you, oh no. We evidently made them believe we had demons because we were so silly laughing so hard that they poured oil in their hands and just smeared it over our forehead and arms. They would be speaking in tongues like there was no tomorrow. "You are going to be saved and delivered right now tonight," they would seem to be saying by the expression on their faces. We didn't know what "saved" was or what we had to be "saved from" so we didn't know how to respond. After so many Friday nights we found out that if we did not act like we got the Spirit by speaking in tongues, crying, shouting or making some kind of sign that God had touched us, we would be in that circle every Friday until the sun came up! I thought I was going to play games with them one night but when they laid hands on me, I fell down to my knees under the power of God and could not stop crying, *"Thank you Jesus for saving me."* My Aunt Bee really started shoutin' because I made a sign. Little did I know that sign marked my life for ministry and the anointing that overshadowed me that night tripped an alarm in satan's kingdom.

I grew up thinking something was wrong about me because everybody said something was different about me but could not tell me what it was. The first target the enemy attacks is your confidence and self-esteem to bruise my heel. First of all, I was extraordinarily taller than everyone wherever I went. By the time I was a teenager, I was already taller than all three of my brothers, my five sisters and even my mother and father. So when God called me to preach, this spirit had already followed me around saying, *"Something is wrong with you; you're different. You're not like everybody else. Don't say nothing, shrink back and act like you don't know if they ask you. Even though you know, don't say anything because they will accuse you of being a show off and will say you think you're all that because of what you know!"* To my own demise, I listened to the voice of the serpent in the garden of my mind (in heavenly places) that held me back from stepping up at the right time when I was before the right people. Missed opportunities are lost when we listen to the enemy and allow the enemy to bruise our heel.

A BRUISED HEEL

When God called me to preach I told him, "I have never heard or seen a woman preach" and I cannot speak in front of a crowd of people, you know I get nervous. Don't you remember when I had to give an oral presentation at Michiana College of Commerce in the class you urged me to take and how my knees were knocking so hard?" He said, "Yes, and out of your belly flowed rivers of living water and the whole class stood up and gave you a standing ovation – Preach the gospel! Be instant in season and out of season!" was His reply! But then I kept crying and went on to tell Him most preachers come from a family line of preachers and my father is not by any means a preacher of the Gospel so I am not qualified." It is often mentioned at our annual family reunions that my father was called to be a preacher and would preach all the time while picking cotton. Because he would preach all the time, they gave him the nickname "Preacher!" Everybody that knew my father, and he was quite popular in the city, called him by his nickname preacher, but not referencing a religious character. After voicing all of my reasons to God why I could not possibly be called to preach, He replied, *"Your father's name is Preacher and the mantle is passed onto you."* God really has a sense of humor, He laughed and I laughed and that settled it so I accepted my call by God to God. I was not going to announce it before the church like everyone else; I was too scared of the Baptist Deacon Board. No woman had ever preached at that church.

Your acceptance of the call to the work of the ministry will be made to God before you confess to your Pastor and profess your calling before the congregation. This is where the seed of satan has bruised the heel of women with the seed of rejection. Seeds produce after their own kind. The seed of rejection produces a spirit of rejection that forms a root of insecurity, fear, low self-image, lack of confidence, and fear. Millions of women received a bruised heel from the seed of being told "to keep silent in the Church." "God does not call women to leadership over a man," is what we have been told.

The enmity between the seed of satan and the seed of the woman intensifies when a woman has a calling on her life to preach the Gospel. While working at a local church in my growth and development stage as a young minister on the roster, one of the members of the church died and the Pastor called for all of the ministers to attend the funeral. I will never forget how the Pastor of that church stood up and embarrassed all the women preachers asking for all the preachers to stand up. When he saw me stand up he pointedly with his voice said, "All of the MALE preachers." And I shrunk back down in my seat trying my best not to cry over the embarrassment. After the service it was one of the deacons from my church who and then my Pastor who came outside to console me and said, "That's all right, you know who you are and he should not have done that to you." My Pastor said, "Deb, don't let that get to you. I'll tell any man in here that you are one of the best preachers I have." Those were all kind words and I needed that encouragement. I was trying to hide my humiliation and act like I was all right, but on the inside my spirit was hurt and weeping. This marked a place in my genesis where the enemy again bruised my heel to keep me from stepping outside of my comfort zone, so instead, I stayed behind and pushed everybody else to the front line. I kept saying to myself that I would just be a help mete to the Pastors and lend my time and assistance to help them build these ministries and I was all right with that. Kept me off the enemy's radar and I could just "have church" and enjoy the fellowship – I thought.

I really enjoyed being everybody's Church Secretary because I was in my career then employed as a Legal Secretary since graduating from MCC. In 1996 I started a company, MCO Publications ("My Church Office") that extended my ability to help even more Pastors. I thought I was safe but God kept calling my name saying, "Preach the Gospel Be Instant Season and Out of Season. Out of your belly shall flow rivers of living water."

I went home and fell upon my bed crying out to God to remove the pain, the shame, and the embarrassment. But it grew up with me and caused my spirit to hide for cover, to silence my voice, to act like I didn't really know what God was saying and doing because those words, "the MALE preachers only" would not let me stand up to represent Christ's authority and identity in me. This is the seed of satan that the enemy has used to bruise the heel of the woman as a stronghold to cause her walk to be halted!

In the 21st Century, Apostolic Women Birthing Nations are awakening to the prophetic revelation of destroying the seed of satan to the set time of the Word of the Lord:

In that day, saith the LORD, will I assemble her that halteth,
and I will gather her that is driven out, and her that I have afflicted;
7And I will make her that halted a remnant, and her that was cast
far off a strong nation: and the LORD shall reign over them in
Mount Zion from henceforth, even for ever.
8And thou, O tower of the flock, the strong hold of the daughter of
Zion, unto thee shall it come, even the first dominion; the kingdom
shall come to the daughter of Jerusalem.
Micah 4:6-9

PRONOUNCEMENT OF THE MANDATE: DAVID BROUGHT DOWN THE HEAD OF GOLIATH WHO WAS SPEAKING AGAINST THE GOD OF ISRAEL. APOSTOLIC WOMEN WILL BRING DOWN THE HEAD OF THE SPIRIT OF RELIGION THAT HAS BRUISED THEIR HEEL AND TRIED TO SILENCE THEIR VOICE.

For this cause are the Sons of God manifest:
To destroy the works of the devil!

I CAME TO SHAKE NATIONS AND TO SUBDUE KINGDOMS!

This is what a court trial transcript from OUR MEDIATOR, ADVOCATE, HIGH PRIEST, SHEPHERD AND CHIEF BISHOP OF OUR SOULS would look like:

Truth is hard to accept when religion has so shaped our belief systems. It has been a long held traditional religious belief that women should “keep silent in the church” and under no circumstance should they be found preaching in the pulpit! To separate the role of women to be called and used by God to function in any one of the five-fold ministry gifts for the perfecting of the saints, for the work of the ministry, for the edifying of the body of Christ based on prima facie evidence is preposterous! The religious spirit has supported this false teaching taken totally out of context from Paul’s statement to the Corinthian church relying solely on prima facie evidence! Legally speaking in accordance with the definition as given by Black’s Law Dictionary, (abridged 7th Edition), “Prima facie” is a Latin expression meaning *“on its first encounter, first blush, or at first sight.”* The literal translation would be "at first face" or "at first appearance," from the feminine form of primus ("first") and facies ("face,") both in the ablative case. It is used in modern legal English to signify that on first examination, “a matter appears to be” self-evident from the facts. In common law jurisdictions, prima facie denotes evidence that – unless rebutted – would be sufficient to prove a particular proposition or fact. The term is used similarly in academic philosophy. Most legal proceedings require a prima facie case to exist, following which proceedings may then commence to test it, and create a ruling" (Wikipedia). To use prima facie evidence in the case of women being kept silent in the 21st Century is preposterous and the religious spirit cannot and will no longer be tolerated. *"If your context is wrong, your conclusion will be wrong"* (statement made by Dr. Cindy Trimm).

By contextually misinterpreting the Apostle Paul's admonishing the men to tell their women not to talk because of the false heretical teachings that were being presented by false teachers at that time. The women were "talking about it" and being too loud in the service. Second, by hanging prima facie evidence on what appeared to be evidence to support those who continue to stand against women as their basis for denying their role as "spiritual fathers" to "help those women" who have an apostolic mandate in God's plan for the redemption of all of mankind "to crush the head of the enemy" (Gen. 3:15)! It is preposterous (i.e., extremely unreasonable or silly) to continue to hold on to this foolish religious belief! We have already refused to be silent! This continued teaching is way behind the times. IT will be silenced in the 21st Century! Throw your head back and say, "Thank you Jesus, it's about time somebody put it to rest! LOL! As the nations will witness the execution of apostolic authority given to Apostles to judge the house of God whenever there is disorder, pass sentences and issue verdicts as John Eckhardt reveals in his book, *The Ministry Anointing of The Apostle* (Eckhardt).

Furthermore, there is not one preacher on earth today who does not preach from, rely and lean heavily upon the Apostle Paul's letters written to the churches to support their sermonic thesis. Paul's letters were sent to birth a movement and to build up the Household of Faith. Paul wrote a third of the New Testament, yet we will probably never hear those who carry this religious spirit mention Paul's letter to the Philippian church about helping those women! For the record we cite Paul's message written in Philippians 4:1-4:

Therefore, my brothers dearly beloved and longed for, my joy and crown, so stand fast in the Lord, my dearly beloved. I beseech Euodias, and beseech Syntyche, that they be of the same mind in the Lord. And I entreat you also, true yoke fellow, help those women which labored with me in the gospel, with Clement also, and with other my fellow laborers, whose names are in the book of life.

Further, in most legal proceedings, one party has a burden of proof, which requires it to present prima facie evidence for all of the essential facts in its case. If they cannot, its claim may be dismissed without any need for a response by other parties. A prima facie case might not stand or fall on its own; if an opposing party introduces other evidence or asserts an affirmative defense it can only be reconciled with a full trial.

The bible is laced with other evidence that can be presented to prove the traditional false teachings of the religious spirit concerning women keeping silent in the church. In fact, the messages about great women throughout the Bible like Esther, Mary, Deborah, Ruth, Hannah, Ana the Prophetess, the woman at the well, the woman with the issue of blood are the very messages they preach the most. Women in the Bible can be preached about but women today should keep silent?

- **If women were to "keep" silent in the church** – the rocks would cry out!
- **If women were to "keep silent in the church"** – there would be no church since women make up 92% of those who attend.
- **If women were to "keep silent in the church"** – there would be no choir, no praise team, no ushers, no greeters, no announcements, no prayer, no TITHES AND OFFERINGS since statistics have proven historically and in the 21st Century women attend more often and therefore give more often than do men.

The affirmative defense would call the message "they" preach whose voice of their generations of sons and daughters who have emerged as powerful men and women of God in the 21st Century. Again, it is preposterous to do 21st Century ministry holding on to these false beliefs. To separate the role of women to be called and used by God to function in any one of the five-fold ministry gifts for the perfecting of the saints, for the work of the ministry, for the edifying of the body of Christ based on prima facie evidence is preposterous exhausted by each and every affirmative defense stated.

FINALLY, man's opinion is of no consequence to the wisdom of God and our submission to the AUTHORITY OF GOD HIMSELF as spoken by the Apostles in Acts: 4:19-20: But Peter and John answered and said unto them, Whether it be right in the sight of God to hearken unto you more than unto God, judge ye. For WE CANNOT BUT SPEAK the things which we have seen and heard (Acts 4:20).

IT IS HEREBY ORDERED, ADJUDGED AND DECREED that this Court finds both men and women who have been called, sanctified, anointed, and sent to preach the gospel of the Kingdom and who have testimonies to show the nation that bear witness to the pain, suffering, persecution, birth pangs and perseverance that is required to preach the Gospel that they are under the same conviction as expressed by The Apostle Paul in I Corinthians 9:6: *"For though I preach the gospel, I have nothing to glory of: for NECESSITY IS LAID UPON ME; YEA, WOE IS UNTO ME, IF I PREACH NOT THE GOSPEL!"*

I REST MY CASE. THIS COURT SHOULD HAVE BEEN ADJOURNED 400 YEARS AGO BETWEEN THE YEARS OF SILENCE BETWEEN THE OLD TESTAMENT AND THE NEW TESTAMENT.

CASE DISMISSED

Chapter 3:

THE REBIRTH OF A NATION AGAINST RELIGIOUS STRONGHOLDS

"But when he, the Spirit of truth, is come, he will guide you into all truth: for he shall not speak of himself; but whatsoever he shall hear, that shall he speak: and he will show you things to come"
(John 16:13)

PROPHETIC PRONOUNCEMENT: GOD USED THE SEED OF A WOMAN IN HIS PLAN OF SALVATION, STEPPING DOWN THROUGH FOURTEEN GENERATIONS THEN, AND HE IS STILL USING THE PROPHETIC VOICE OF A WOMAN TO SPEAK IN OUR GENERATIONS NOW!

As noted previously, the truth is hard to accept when religion has so shaped our belief systems. A revelation of truth shifts paradigms that produces wisdom and knowledge whether it "lines up with our system of theological persuasion or not. The religious spirit always demands revelation to "line up with" its own interpretation for confirmation which mindset believes it has the authority to affirm and approve as though they wrote it. One of the keys of apostolic ministry is the unlocking of the mysteries of the church. There are many hidden mysteries that the 21st Century church will be given to advance the Kingdom that go against religious strong holds to break the power that holds back the truth in a lie.

BEHOLD I SHOW YOU A MYSTERY:
How long wilt thou go about, O thou backsliding daughter?
for the LORD hath created a new thing in the earth,
A woman shall compass a man"
Jeremiah 31:22, KJV

Apostolic women are birthing nations through the womb in this time for a specific purpose by the Holy Ghost to destroy the works of the enemy that have bruised her heel. The Geneva Study Bible comments on this scripture that, *"Because their deliverance from Babylon was a figure of their deliverance from sin, he shows how this would be procured that is, by Jesus Christ, whom a woman would conceive and bear in her womb,"* which is a strange thing in the earth, because He would be born of a virgin without man. Jerusalem which was like a barren woman in her captivity would be fruitful as she that is joined in marriage and whom God blesses with children.

Against every religious stronghold that has caused women to halt in a backslidden position, the "new thing" that God has created is Apostolic Women! They are birthing nations that are not confined, contained or controlled by a ministry inside the four walls of a church building. This structure and foundation controls their movement and restricts their true calling and purpose. Apostolic women are building businesses as entrepreneurs; building churches, schools, ministries, websites for economic commerce; delivering technologies; raising the level in church administration; ministering to the single parents, prostitutes, married women, divorced women; helping families in shelters; starting transitional living homes for men coming out of prison institutions, and more! They are more representative in number and supplying the finances and resources for mission fields across continents – that's apostolic – i.e. "sent" (apostellos) into all nations preaching, teaching, healing the sick and raising the dead! Great ministries are being birthed through women of God who are being sent to nations like Asia, India, Ghana and Africa. They are building orphanages in Kenya and creating sustainable methods for delivering food to villages and feeding the poor. That's Apostolic!

Apostolic ministry is a pioneering and building ministry that repairs foundations and removes old structures that keep the church from advancing. As an apostolic builder and architect, it is easier for you to see the structure, assess the damage, and allow God to give you a blueprint for restoration. What is difficult is to penetrate the deep seated spirit of religion and uproot the Jezebel spirit of control.

Chapter 4:

POST- MODERNISM AND POST-CHRISTIANITY IN THE 21ST CENTURY

Living in a Post-Modern world in an age of Post-Christianity, we cannot afford to acknowledge nor choose to ignore the Issachar anointing that God has released over the nations as a 21st Century guide for 21st Century ministry. Attempting to function in the Gifts of the Spirit with a carnal and religious mindset will be ineffective.

"Personal world views, ideologies, religious movements or societies that are no longer rooted in the language and assumptions of Christianity, at least explicitly, though it had previously been in an environment of ubiquitous Christianity (i.e., Christendom). The 21st Century has superimposed a post-Christian set of belief systems in which Christianity is no longer the dominant civil religion, and has gradually assumed values, culture, and worldviews that are not necessarily Christian (and further may not necessarily reflect any world religion's standpoint, or may represent a combination of either several religions or none). Post-modernism is characterized by the decline of Christianity, particularly in Europe, Canada, and Australia in the 20th and 21st centuries. Post-Modernism is used pejoratively to describe writers, artists, or critics who give the impression they believe in no absolute truth or objective reality. Generally, therefore, post-Christian tends to refer to the loss of Christianity's monopoly, if not its followers, in historically Christian societies. In his *1961 **The Death of God**,* the French theologian Gabriel Vahanian argued that modern secular culture in most of Western Civilization had lost all sense of the sacred, lacked any sacramental meaning, and disdained any transcendental purpose or sense of providence, bringing him to the conclusion that for the modern mind, "God is dead." Some American Christians (primarily Protestants) also use this term in reference to the evangelism of unChurched individuals who may have grown up in a non-Christian culture where traditional Biblical references may be unfamiliar concepts amongst previous generations in the United States (Wikipedia, "Post Christianity.")

Consequently, while post-modern worldviews are emerging a violent and radical polarization and characterization of the relevance of the Christian faith that challenge the authority of the Word of God, there is a quickening of the Spirit of the Lord emerging within the 21st Century Church. The scriptures from Genesis to Revelation have foretold the coming of this age that gives this emerging body of Believers a charge to *"Be not conformed to this world: but be ye transformed by the renewing of your mind, that ye may prove what is that good, and acceptable, and perfect, will of God"* not the good and perfect will of man's carnal desires nor opinions.

Interesting to note that against the cultural shifting and SHIFTING of worldviews in the 21st Century concerning biblical truths that we hold as absolute truth, political, religious and counter philosophical imaginations attempt to take God out of the equation through deception and vain imaginations for nations to exist absent with God. I still believe in the authority and inerrancy of scripture and that it is still relevant and necessary to understanding this SHIFT in worldviews. In this time of reformation, it is the greatest time to come into the knowledge of the truth amidst critical and postmodern thought and vain philosophies which give rise to the nations anti-Christ movements. In order for believers to advance the Kingdom of God in an apostate, post-modern and post-Christian age, our guide for 21st Century ministry should be what Paul instructs the Colossian church to do:

"Beware lest any man spoil you through philosophy and vain deceit,
after the tradition of men,
after the rudiments of the world, and not after Christ"
Colossians 2:8, KJV

Chapter 5:

WHEN KINGDOMS COLLIDE

The kingdoms of the world and the Kingdom of Heaven both have their own set of governmental rule, authority and power that dictate, shape and form our existence and survival within seven areas that influence our culture: business, government, media, arts and entertainment, education, the family and religion. Because religion is "any system of belief that adheres to its own specific set of doctrines and practices and claims to be unique," when the mountain of religion collides with the Kingdom, belief systems and mindsets bring conflict to traditional, long held, iron clad ideals and values. The church has held these long-standing beliefs and mindsets high. Thus, resulting in birth pangs of a nation. When change is demanded and the time is eminent, new leadership, new technologies, new things, new discoveries in medicine, science, geography, mathematics and learning all relative to the seven spheres (business, government, media, arts and entertainment, education, family, and religion) will emerge to SHIFT a nation forward that many will resist.

For example, in the 21st Century during our process of election for the next President of the United States, the U.S. Constitution and the framing words written by our American forefathers centuries ago, have been challenged many times just recently. These issues affect all of the seven areas of influence today, especially religious beliefs and constitutional rights to bear arms against as we face the problems of our world today. Many people get stuck in time when God is moving in time to fulfill a greater purpose for our existence. Religion has kept us stuck in time on issues pertaining to the call of ministry and the purpose of the existence of the church. Ultimately, the authority of the Lordship of Christ and kingdom rule superimposes practices of religious indoctrination of systematic theology.

SYSTEMATIC THEOLOGY

Systematic theology is a discipline of Christian theology that attempts to formulate an orderly, rational, and coherent account of the Christian faith and beliefs. It is also called dogmatics, which is the systematic study of church dogmas - a statement, opinion, forcibly asserted as if authoritative and unchallengeable based on assumption rather than empirical observation. Categorically defined, "systematic theology draws on the foundational sacred texts of Christianity, while simultaneously investigating the development of Christian doctrine over the course of history, particularly through philosophy, science and ethics." Inherent to a system of theological thought is that a method is developed, one which can be applied both broadly and particularly. The setting out of the varied ideas of Christianity (and the various topics and themes of the diverse texts of the Bible) in a single, coherent and well-ordered presentation is a relatively late development.

In Eastern Orthodoxy, an early example is provided by John of Damascus's 8th-century Exposition of the Orthodox Faith, in which he attempts to set in order, and demonstrate the coherence of, the theology of the classic texts of the Eastern theological tradition. In the West, Peter Lombard's 12th-century Sentences, in which he collected thematically a large series of quotations from the Church Fathers, became the basis of a medieval scholastic tradition of thematic commentary and explanation - best exemplified in Thomas Aquinas's Summa Theologica. The Lutheran scholastic tradition of a thematic, ordered exposition of Christian theology emerged in the 16th century, with Philipp Melanchthon's Loci Communes, and was countered by a Calvinist scholasticism, exemplified by John Calvin's Institutes of the Christian Religion. According to some theologians in evangelical circles, it is used to refer to the topical collection and exploration of the content of the Bible, in which a different perspective is provided on the Bible's message than that garnered simply by reading the biblical narratives, poems, proverbs, and letters as a story of redemption or as a manual for how to live a godly life. One advantage of this approach is that it allows one to see all that the Bible says regarding some subject (e.g. the attributes of God), and one danger is a tendency to assign technical definitions to terms based on a few passages and then read that meaning everywhere the term is used in the Bible (e.g.

"justification" as Paul uses it in his letter to the Romans) is allegedly different from how James uses it in his letter (Romans 4:25, Romans 5:16-18 and James 2:21-25). In this view, systematic theology is complementary to biblical theology. Biblical theology traces the themes chronologically through the Bible, while systematic theology examines themes topically; biblical theology reflects the diversity of the Bible, while systematic theology reflects its unity" (Wikipedia, "Systematic Theology.")

Chapter 6:

THE ABUSE OF POWER BY LEADERS

A master of deception appeared in the garden of our genesis then and has appeared in our garden of redemption today! Deception in the garden from the beginning is the deception in the garden today through the abuse of power and suggestion to violate the will of God. Deception comes in many forms and filters its evil intent through information and technology devised to steal plans, abort purposes and ultimately to destroy God's original intent. Deception and identity theft through technology revolution in the 21st Century has given rise to the ability to create a profile "image" as a marketing tool to brand a person or company's "image" in order to attract business. As prophecy continues to unfold, we understand the prophecy given by the Prophet

"But thou, O Daniel, shut up the words, and seal the book, even to the time of the end:
many shall run to and fro, and knowledge shall be increased
Daniel 12:4, KV

Technology has given the nations the ability for knowledge to be increased changing communications has removed barriers to access information across nations. Our landscape is now global which has opened the doors and windows to nations through the use of the Internet to do business and ministry with in a way we could not have perceived forty years ago. As much as we resisted the technological change that we saw coming, change was eminent and the time had come. Nothing or no one could stop it.

I remember when cell phones were first introduced and it seemed impossible to be able to walk around outside or be riding in your car with the ability to talk on the telephone. Phone booths are now obsolete and the use of those huge telephone books we used to depend on have been replaced by Internet search engines such as Google and are now a thing of the past. The 21st Century has brought the nation into an era of advancement, acceleration of time, and increase of knowledge mainly through technology and an ever changing of the fabric of our society in the areas of family, business, government, arts, entertainment, and religion. Ideas and values have changed and we have SHIFTED into a new dimension in the realm of the Spirit where heaven is invading earth with miraculous signs, wonders and the working of mighty miracles through the hands of the Apostles and Prophets in this Kingdom Age.

THE ENEMY'S USE OF LEADERS TO BRUISE THE HEEL

Satan has for generations used religious false teachers dark shadows by leaders who mirror a very evil and hostile projection of the enemy's M.O. (method of operation) of their followers and supporters. As God cursed the serpent in the garden, the enemy's attitude towards women has been targeted to bruise her identity and debunk (i.e., to reduce the reputation of someone by ridicule, scandal and if necessary through extreme lies) her authority in order to destroy the seed she carries to birth nations (Genesis 3:15). Enemy is defined as "a person who feels hatred for, fosters harmful designs against, or engages in antagonistic activities against another; an adversary or opponent; an armed foe; an opposing military force: a hostile nation or state; a citizen of such a state; enemies, persons, nations, etc., that are hostile to one another" (www.dictionary.com). This dark and shadowy mirrors the image definition of an enemy as a person is reflective pattern of traits that characterize the attitudes, actions and behaviors of "persons" found mainly in leadership roles who are found in seats of authority in Government, business, education, marketplace, the employment, and worst, in seats of authority in the church posed as religious leaders who exercise and abuse their power and authority.

In my undergrad class on Christians Business Ethics at LeTourneau University, we studied through a book entitled, "Meeting the Ethical Challenges of Leadership-Second Edition" by Craig E. Johnson (2005). Johnson describes how leaders cast light or shadows through five types of power bases: 1) Coercive Power is based on penalties or punishments like physical force, salary reductions, student suspensions, or embargoes against national enemies; 2) Reward Power depends on being able to deliver something of value to others, whether tangible (bonuses, health insurance, grades) or intangible (praise, trust cooperation); 3) Legitimate Power resides in the position, not the person. Supervisors, judges, police officers, instructors, and parents have the right to control our behavior within certain limits. A boss can require us to carry out certain tasks at work, for example, but in most cases, he or she has no say in what we do in our free time. In contrast to legitimate power, expert power is based on the characteristics of the individual, regardless of his or her official position. Knowledge, skills, education, and certification in one's field all build what is known as 4) Expert Power and 5) Reverent Power rests on the admiration one individual has for another.

The abusive use of these powers and shadows of death that have been cast over the nations by leaders have been used by the enemy to bruise the heel of the men and women in ministry especially and the violently in the workplace. The battle of the seed for the seat of power has continued since the garden because ultimately as it is written: "The seed of the woman will crush the head of the enemy!" Whoever controls the head controls the mind.

Chapter 7:

UNMASKING THE DISGUISE OF PSYCHOPATHIC DECEPTION

"The great masses of people will more easily fall victims to a big lie than to a small one."
-Adolph Hitler

For many Believers and "church goers" who have shut their eyes to the truth that not everyone who "goes to church" or who are connected with our prayer lines and teleconferences, or are "regular" attendees at our "church" events are born again, saved and spirit filled. I have to agree with Dr. Hare and Dr. Cleckley that "most of these people are not just right in your churches, schools, charitable organizations, and workplaces, but by their very nature, they are likely running them." The need for absolute power over others and the wish to inflict pain for the enjoyment of watching others suffer, are almost never apparent to the casual observer. The reason for this is that another core trait of the psychopath is disguise. So unfortunately, these individuals usually mask themselves as good-natured people. "This outward appearance," says Dr. Cleckley, is essentially a mask, which, "may include business or professional careers that continue in a sense successful, and which are truly successful when measured by financial reward or by the casual observer's opinion of real accomplishment" (The Hidden Evil).

Just as it is the enemy's M.O. is to deceive by masking as a Prophet as "wolves in sheep's clothing but inwardly they are ravening wolves (Matthew 7:15, KJV) in order to position himself in core positions of leadership and key positions of influence, his true motive is not to serve but it is as always to kill, steal and to destroy. The most important guide for 21st ministry is to Beware of false Prophets, who come to you in sheep's clothing. We know the enemy will come in greater disguise in this time of Kingdom advance and reformation because of the weight of God's glory that has been increasing and the spirit of wickedness in the nations has been increasing.

"And because iniquity shall abound, the love of many shall wax cold. But he that shall endure unto the end, the same shall be saved. And this gospel of the kingdom shall be preached in all the world for a witness unto all nations; and then shall the end come (Matthew 24:12-14).

A master of deception appeared in the garden of our genesis then and has appeared in our garden of redemption today! In "The Mask of Sanity," written by Hervey Milton Cleckley, M.D. (1903 - January 28, 1984), an American psychiatrist and pioneer in the field of psychopathy, it is distinguished by his central thesis that the psychopath exhibits normal function according to standard psychiatric criteria, yet privately engages in destructive behavior. Psychopath is the idea of a master deceiver secretly possessed of no moral or ethical restraints, yet behaving in public with excellent function (Wikipedia). Cleckley, says that psychopaths are always able to justify their actions, no matter how brutal. They have, "an ability to rationalize their behavior so that "it appears" warranted, reasonable, and justified." Dr. Robert Hare, in his book, "Without Conscience" added, "Psychopaths show a stunning lack of concern for the devastating effects their actions have on others. Often they are completely forthright about the matter, calmly stating that they have no sense of guilt, [and] are not sorry for the pain and destruction they have caused," which, is associated with a remarkable ability to rationalize their behavior. Lying, deceiving, and manipulation are natural talents for psychopaths. When caught in a lie or challenged with the truth, they are seldom perplexed or embarrassed--they simply "change their stories" or attempt to rework the facts so that they "appear" to be consistent with the lie. When God cursed the serpent in the Garden and said, *"Upon your belly you shall eat the dust of the earth,"* indicates that satan once walked upright before he trespassed in the Garden of Eden!

> PROPHETIC PRONOUNCEMENT: THE VOICE OF THE LORD IS WALKING AGAIN 'IN THE COOL OF THE GARDEN' CALLING ONCE AGAIN TO HIS CREATION AGAINST THE VOICE OF THE ENEMY "ADAM, WHERE ARE YOU?"

THE FALL

The fall of man in the garden was more than a fall in the weakness of the flesh! Our mindset has been conditioned by the religious spirit to have us to believe that when a person falls, they fall because they "backslid" and fell into sin by the works of the flesh by an action or behavior that is frowned upon by the religious self-righteous concluding they are not saved anymore. I remember when my cousin on my father's side (C.O.G.I.C.) went to a movie and it was told to our family (my mother's side, BAPTIST) that she fell and has backslidden because she went to a movie and was seen wearing a short dress, big earrings and red lipstick! Can you believe that?! As a thirteen year old girl, that puzzled me. I loved my cousin dearly because she was two years older than I was, and I looked up to her because she said she would teach me how to be a big girl. I wanted to be a big girl! The big girl lesson she taught me was to "stay away from mannish horny little boys who will try their best to get in your pants!" She was so cool and funny and could dance. To hear the family talk about her with such disgrace grieved my little spirit. I could not understand how going to a movie, wearing a short dress, big earrings and red lipstick made a person a sinner fallen from the love and grace of God. Me, always for the underdog, defended her and was told I'm too young to understand and don't be hangin' around with her. I understood the church frowned on her and made a big deal about it when she went to church. She wasn't a "holier than thou" saint, but to me, she wasn't a sinner just for that!

We kept hangin' and keeping it real! Amazing how mortal men become the judge and jury rendering verdict of whose saved and whose not based on the works of the flesh. The Lord revealed to me to understand that it is the Spirit of a man that sustains him, the flesh profits nothing. We have a tendency to judge by the flesh and not by the Spirit. The lies we are told and the consequence of those who wear the psychopathic mask of deception "appearing" in our lives with hidden agendas and false motives have caused many of the righteous to fall since the beginning, especially during the 21st Century. It is the gift of discernment that must be elevated to truly identify with honor and respect those that God has pregnant to birth purpose in this 21st Century.

The casting of the shadow of death that destroys visions and dreams is released when you listen to the voice of the enemy that shows up in your garden suggesting that what you are seeing is not really of God. The devil's deception has led many to believe that somehow you must "attack" by coming against ministries, especially the newborns, to destroy, because you believe you have the right to do so. Many have fallen by your own evil conscience. There is only one voice to hear and that is the voice of the Holy Spirit.

"Many are the afflictions of the righteous: but the LORD delivereth him out of them all"
Psalms 34:19

Part Two

THE BIRTH PANGS OF RECOVERY

Chapter 8:

THROUGH MULTIPLIED SORROWS

Unto the woman he said, I will greatly multiply your sorrow and your conception; in sorrow you shall bring forth children; and your desire shall be to your husband, and he shall rule over you.
Genesis 3:15

Because what you are carrying has the power to impact nations on many levels of business, education, media, the arts, entertainment, family and religion, it will not be a walk in the park. Keep in mind that the battle for the seed of purpose is the battle for dominion, rule, and power that was given in your genesis (beginning). The apostolic anointing to birth nations will multiply your sorrows by the attacks of the enemy. After battling the abuse of power by leaders and the spirit of religion, the closer the time comes to birth purpose, the more sorrows seem to multiply. It's challenging in the 21st Century with so many distractions vying for our attention to get us off purpose. I was telling a young woman who is being repositioned for the next level of ministry that ministry will make you cry. She was on assignment as a prayer intercessor for our 24-hour prayer watch; she was scheduled to come up and pray between 10:00 pm and 11:00pm. At the time she was to carry out her assignment, in her own process of birthing her ministry to the next level, a series of attacks was set against her mind. Various distractions stood up against her. Whenever you come to the time of birthing nations, you will have to press through to breakthrough! It is the natural process of birthing called "contractions" that we identify as distractions. These birth pangs are the beginning of sorrows.

One true test of an apostle is the level of warfare he or she experiences that brings sorrow and tears through pain to the point of wanting to give up and die - but you can't! Have you ever felt like you were walking dead? That's the garden where your sweat falls as great drops of blood like Jesus cried, *"Father, if it be thy will take this cup from me. But, nevertheless thy will be done."* We have all desired to go to the next level, and I remember one day God spoke and asked me, *"Can You Drink of the Cup?"* I paused and pondered the question because I didn't know, and had not yet tasted the bitterness of the cup. Our minds cannot conceive what it takes to get to the next level in God. We shout, dance and sing and get excited about the glimpse of glory that we see. But when God begins to take you to the next level, you really want to say, *"I'm sorry I ever asked God to take me to the next level."*

The next level is apostolic warfare training being driven into the wilderness to be tempted of the devil. After that it is up the Villa DeLarosa carrying a cross as Jesus did not a video camera to post on YouTube! God's ordination and calling of the Apostle and Prophet is sanctioned and sealed before anybody ever laid hands on you, licensed or ordained, or affirmed you. Your degree, your Certificate of License and Ordination will pale in comparison to the reality of the "Oath" you took when you were installed as a five-fold ministry Gift to the Body of Christ for the level of ministry needed in the 21st Century! Listen to the mentor in Paul describe how he felt as an Apostle while doing "the work of the ministry" when he came to the next level of crushing the enemy's head and bringing reformation, building the church, laying a new foundation in the faith against the works of the religious Pharisees, Sadducees, false Prophets, false Apostles and false teachers:

"For we would not, brethren, have you ignorant of our trouble which came to us in Asia, that we were pressed out of measure, above strength, insomuch that we despaired even of life: But we had the sentence of death in ourselves, that we should not trust in ourselves, but in God which raiseth the dead"
II Corinthians 1:3-9

Your comfort, and most of the time, your only comfort will be The Father! This anointing to be steadfast and unmovable always abounding in the work of the Lord comes through birth pangs of multiplied sorrow for both males and females to deliver the seed that is going to crush the enemy's head. When I was "confirmed" (emphasis added) to the Office of Apostle, my sorrow was multiplied and so shall it be for the new wineskins to birth nations, bring deliverance, set the captives free in a time of reformation.

Chapter 9:

THE BIRTHING OF FULLY PERSUADED! MINISTRIES INTERNATIONAL

The enemy does not fight you for where you are – he fights you for where you are going! The ministry you are carrying to birth nations is the seed of the woman to bring forth a Son, a nation that will be delivered by the power of the Holy Ghost that is growing inside of you. From the time that God births a vision in you until the time it fully manifest, the enemy is watching your Prophetic time clock ready to devour:

REVELATION 12:1-6
"And there appeared A GREAT WONDER IN HEAVEN; A WOMAN clothed with the sun, and the moon under her feet, and upon her head a crown of twelve stars: 2And she being with child cried, travailing in birth, and pained to be delivered.

And there "appeared" another wonder in heaven; and behold a great red dragon, having seven heads and ten horns, and seven crowns upon his heads. And HIS TAIL DREW THE THIRD PART OF THE STARS OF HEAVEN, and did cast them to the earth: and the dragon stood before the woman which was ready to be delivered, for TO DEVOUR HER CHILD AS SOON AS IT WAS BORN"

And she brought forth a man child, who was to rule all nations with a rod of iron: and her child was caught up unto God, and His throne.
And the woman fled into the wilderness, WHERE SHE HATH A PLACE PREPARED OF GOD, that they should feed her there a thousand two hundred and threescore days"

The seed of satan has birthed a national, regional and global counterfeit network and Schools of the Prophets that look like you, dress like you, shout and praise like you, sing and dance, prophesy, praise, have prophetic minstrels like you – but they are not like you! They have a form of godliness but their motive is like their father the devil (John 8:44). Read the parable of the sower *revelationally* with this fact in mind. There are two seeds in the earth, the seed of good and the seed of evil. There are wheat and there are tares and the tares come up to choke the wheat. It all depends on what kind of ground (i.e., foundation) it is planted in and the origin of the seed that has been sown. You cannot just go to any church. You cannot cast your pearls before swine! Your time is seed. Your talents are seed. Your financial giving is seed and you could be putting your money into a bag of holes. Whenever you make an investment in good ground, it will produce a good harvest (see, The Parable of the Sower, Mark 4:1-20). More importantly, you can only connect with Divine Kin-nections. I like to spell it that way because it denotes "kinship" in relationships.

THROW JEZEBEL OFF THE WALL!

The Jezebel spirit sits in control of the worship, the movement, who gets to serve and who is to be silenced. People fear change and the religious spirit wants everything to remain the same because it thinks it is in control. Nevertheless, the old order must give way to the new order that God is anointing His Body in the 21st Century. It is the anointing that breaks the yoke of bondage of strongholds that is necessary for the rebirthing of nations to thrive and succeed in economic downturns and spiritual complacency.

Many Prophetic ministries are hidden like Elijah was hidden for a season in time as he took shelter in a cave from the threat of Jezebel. Anyone who is casting dark shadows proclaiming death threats against the true Apostles and Prophets of God in this time is sure to find the same fate that Jezebel found when she was thrown off the wall. The Jehu anointing that is upon those who are birthing nations is stronger now than it was in the days of Elijah. We are in the days of "greater works" as Jesus sits at the right hand of the Father ever living to make intercession for His sons and daughters who are called to advance the Kingdom in the 21st Century. God has set this time to throw down Jezebelic Prophets, castrated eunuchs who helped her in the past that will not succeed in the enemy's future. The seed of satan may have bruised your heel, but this time you are going to crush his head!

During this three-year period God began again to speak to me again about the vision of Fully Persuaded Ministries. He took me back to a vision of the coming of the Kingdom He showed in me in 1996 that was designed to shake nations and subdue kingdoms. I always wrote that on my brochures and correspondence not knowing what it meant then but I understand it now. This ministry was to be totally "out of the box" and would change the "order of service" as we know it. He talked to me about the preaching of the Gospel of the Kingdom and that the time was coming when the spirit of religion and tradition would be broken. I sat and wrote the vision for many days. I keep a notepad and ink pen with me at all times because God is always speaking.

I began to hear a sound that was not like the sound I heard inside the sanctuary. This was the sound of heaven and it sounded like a trumpet. I began to tell people that I hear the sound of the voice and the feet of the Apostles and Prophets. After several years they began to emerge and meet in what they called Apostolic Councils and Prophetic Roundtables. I was invited by the Apostles I was sitting under. I was blessed and graced to be in those meetings in the late 90s with great men and women of God in what was like being in the council of nations. Nobody asked me who I was they just acted like I was supposed to be there and talked towards me that way. They came from all over, all races from all denominational backgrounds converging to discuss the new order of the

Kingdom. I could agree with everything they were saying because I had heard God say the same things.

The time had come when they that worship Him must worship Him in Spirit and in Truth which is in the light of their true calling, identity and purpose. The worshippers I saw in the spirit were not like the praise leaders I saw on the "platform" in the flesh worshipping like the woman at the well who Jesus said you worship what you know not John 4:22-24). The vision of a church I saw being birthed out of traditional styles of "church service" were so free in such an atmosphere of liberty that clouds began to fill the room. The atmosphere SHIFTED that released the glory of the Lord and the heavens were opened. This glory was seen and experienced and felt by all. Nobody would be looking around the room or looking down upon those that bowed down and worshipped Him because nobody could do anything except Worship Him!

In 1996 God spoke and said, "Set the atmosphere and I will fill it." Build the ministries that would provide a place of refuge for those who had been hurt and wounded in ministry to be healed and for their gifts and anointing to be activated. A new wineskin is emerging that will bring a strong Apostolic and Prophetic impartation to breathe life back into the Body. You will raise the dead and heal the sick. You will cancel the attack of the enemy that brings strong delusion and reveal counterfeit spirits that disguise themselves to deceive my people. I brought you out to bring you in. It's easy to say yes, but to be made to conform to yes is to drink of the cup! When God brings the 21st Century church to this place of brokenness and healed through repentance, the new wineskins will replace the old wineskins and the bones will live. He reminded me of the message I preached in 1994 "Can these Bones Live" that challenged the religious status quo then but was about to be intensified when I would birth a ministry and deliver an Apostolic and Prophetic message through Fully Persuaded Ministries. God calls you in time ahead of time and shows you a vision that must go through a process of multiplied sorrows. It tries you in the fire so that you will come through as pure gold. The birth pangs of delivery are intensified before the head begins to crown.

OUT OF THE WILDERNESS

After about three years in the wilderness and being in the Prophet's cave hiding from the Jezebel spirit of witchcraft and witnessing the Ahab spirit of Jezebel's control over spiritual leaders, being attacked by the viruses in the Body of Christ, God began the process of healing. It was during this season that I turned down "engagements" because I did not want to preach. Slowly I began to climb out of despairing of life itself and began to realize that one day I would be able to see that this trial came to make me strong. I began to pray fervently. Pastors, Bishops and Apostles were being attacked by four ranking powers that God forewarned me was going to strike the nation: 1) Hostile takeover, 2) Spirit of Deception; 3)

Identity theft, and 4) the Spirit of Sabotage! This would be the enemy's plan to humiliate and bring shame and destroy ministries, business, governments, families, celebrities in the arts, evade the schools and disrupt the world's banking and financial systems. All of these strikes have happened over the last seven years.

November 8, 2009 I launched the ministry in a state of the art, drop down screens, built in sound system, 500-space covered parking garage connected to a movie theatre, a four star hotel accessible by a skywalk located in an affluent, upscale section of the City. Perfect I thought to myself and began to share the vision and show the facilities with everybody just knowing everybody was going to be happy with what God had provided for FPM! It was so much that I thought I could share it with everybody and everybody would be blessed by my blessing. Isn't that what we pray, "God bless me to be a blessing?" People had always told me that I cannot share everything with everybody. I was still naive in believing that everybody who was in ministry were truly the people of God and I was blessed to bless everybody. How naive I was and was rudely AWAKENED to find the opposite to be true.

You are excited when God has given you a vision and then the provision for the vision shows up. Well the vision to be fruitful and multiply, have dominion, subdue the earth was a great vision in the garden too. Not only are those that are to be blessed by your blessing hearing the sound of God's plan of greatness that is coming through you, but the serpent heard it too. Hath God said.....? Isn't a shame how the serpent shows up in your garden and causes the body to attack the body when one part of the body is being blessed because it's their time?

We have all experienced setbacks in our life that seem to happen at the most inopportune time and we say, "Out of all times for this to happen, why now?" This was the question I kept asking God since I had waited since 1996 to deliver FPM, like a pregnant woman has to wait for nine months to deliver a child. Some of you have waited for nine years to birth the ministry God put inside of you, and just when you were about to deliver, just getting ready to start the business, just when your son was graduating from high school, an enemy shows up in the garden waiting to devour as soon as it is born! I had been writing the vision for this ministry since 1996. As soon as I stepped out to deliver, there appeared right where I launched the ministry – a serpent with a pack of wolves in sheep's clothing who set in to devour.

And there appeared a great wonder in heaven; a woman clothed with the sun, and the moon under her feet, and upon her head a crown of twelve stars: And she being with child cried, travailing in birth, and pained to be delivered. And there appeared another wonder in heaven; and behold a great red dragon, having seven heads and ten horns, and seven crowns upon his heads. And his tail drew the third part of the stars of heaven, and did cast them to the earth: and the dragon stood before the woman which was ready to be delivered, for to devour her child as soon as it was born. And she brought forth a man child, who was to rule all nations with a rod of iron: and her child was caught up unto God, and to his throne. And the woman fled into the wilderness, where she hath a place prepared of God, that they should feed her there a thousand two hundred and threescore days (Rev. 12:1-6)

Some of them were "foes" disguised as "friends" who went with me to my graduation ready to devour the attainment of the gift of wisdom and knowledge as I matriculated through LeTourneau School of Professional & Development Studies graduating with honors summa cum laude (which means with highest honors, with highest praise) in June, 2009 ready to write books, start businesses, launch the ministry. Multiplied sorrows came one right after the other through a series of life's struggles.

THE RETICULAR ACTIVATING SYSTEM

Multiplied sorrows will cause your pain to be multiplied when you are birthing a ministry, starting a business, trying to keep your marriage together, pastoring a church, or trying to finish school. I found out that there was a place in me that I never knew or expected to be touched so deep that it would take three years to fully recover from.

According to Innovation and Information for Sustainable Living, this system is considered the brain's attention center. It is the key for switching on your brain and also considered as the main center of motivation. The reticular activating system is connected to the spinal cord at its base from where it accepts information which comes from the ascending sensory tracts directly. It travels up to the mid brain and while going up forms a complex neuron collection that acts as a convergence point for signals from the interior environment as well as the external surroundings. So, the reticular activating system is a place where your thoughts, internal feelings and the outside influences converge. It is very skilled in producing dynamic effects on the motor activity centers located in the brain and the cortex activity such as the frontal lobes. The most important function of reticular activating system is TO REGULATE "THE SHIFT" BETWEEN SLEEP AND WAKEFULNESS (emphasis added).

The transition made by our body from deep slumber to being completely awake as well as functional and vice versa is under the control of this system. It also plays a vital role during our sleep and when we see dreams. It is also responsible for supplying integrated response to the outside stimuli. The skill to sluice (i.e., a sliding gate or other device for controlling the flow of water) out information brought out by the external sources and to pinpoint a particular fact with detailed thought is the controlled effect of the reticular activating system. Coordination while walking, eating or sexual functions are carried out by RAS.

When the enemy especially uses people as his adversaries to abort, block, sabotage, lie, scheme, promote scams to prevent you from bringing forth the glory of God according to the number of the stars that you cannot count, God says I will repay.

In November, 2009 I launched the ministry at the Norris Conference Center, state of the art, drop down screens, built in sound system, covered parking garage connected to The Edwards Theatre, a four star hotel accessible by a sky walk located in the Energy Corridor of the City. Perfect I thought to myself and began to share it with everybody just knowing everybody was going to be happy with what God had provided for FPM! How wrong indeed I found the opposite to be true. The same devil in the garden is the same dragon in Revelations that attacked the mind (in heavenly places)!

For two years prior to launching the ministry I was in the wilderness in a place prepared by God. I could relate to how Elijah felt being threatened with death by the wicked Jezebel, who "calls herself a Prophetess" and what it is like to confront and deal with Prophetic witchcraft (Rev. 2:20). It was here that God begin the process of healing my mind from the attacks of the enemy. The enemy's plan is to frustrate, humiliate and bring shame to any ministry that God sends to birth nations. You should know that the gift to the Office of any of the five-fold ministry gifts to the Body of Christ will cost you everything, even your reputation through false accusations as you fight the enemy of your soul. I told everybody and now the enemy has come in to what it seemed at that time devoured it. I thought the vision that I saw of God building this blueprint and pattern of a ministry and establishing a new order of leadership and worship designed to shake nations and subdue kingdoms was just my vision but it was the vision of a global kingdom arising who was to rule all nations with a rod of iron: and her child was caught up unto God, and to his throne that would crush the enemy's head!

Chapter 10:

REDISCOVERING CHURCH MEMBERSHIP

That we henceforth be no more children, tossed to and fro, and carried about with every wind of doctrine, by the sleight of men, and cunning craftiness, whereby they lie in wait to deceive; But speaking the truth in love, may grow up into him in all things, which is the head, even Christ: From whom the whole body fitly joined together and compacted by that which every joint supplieth, according to the effectual working in the measure of every part, maketh increase of the body unto the edifying of itself in love.
Ephesians 4:14-16

The Kingdom requires a paradigm shift which is not always easy to accept but is most often difficult to hear and to know when the times change to break through the strongholds that hinder the Commission "to make disciples of all nations." It is hard to hear for millions who are experiencing the pain of suffering economically and spiritually today. The Book of Romans speaks to the timing of those who are emerging as apostolic leaders who hear and will answer the cry of suffering as the nation and the church continue in the process of restoration, recovery, and reformation:

For I reckon that the sufferings of this present time are not worthy to be compared with the glory which shall be revealed in us. For the earnest expectation of the creation waits for the manifestation of the Sons of God
Romans 8:19, KJV

The truth is the 21st Century can no longer continue to "have Church" without accepting the truth that such practice does not exist. Where did that concept begin to construct an image of the Body of Christ? When did we start believing that "going to Church" was proof of our salvation and a practice that is mandatory in order for others to believe that we are truly committed to serving God? The statistics of people not going to Church are alarming because they reflect a group of people who are tired of the traditional norm. What they want is A Worship Experience that will deepen their revelation and relationship with God Himself. After that, they cannot go back to church as usual. A time of understanding brings a liberating freedom that you were not called to "work in the Church" set up programs and stay inside the four walls of the building. THE CHURCH IS NOT THE BUILDING! Some will keep "HAVING CHURCH AS USUAL" and never come into the knowledge of the truth. Jesus made a powerful statement about the buildings we worship:

And Jesus went out, and departed from the temple: and his disciples came to him to show him the buildings of the temple.

And Jesus said unto them, See you not all these things? Verily I say unto you, THERE SHALL NOT BE LEFT HERE ONE STONE UPON ANOTHER, THAT SHALL NOT BE THROWN DOWN.
Matthew 24:1-2

Thus says the LORD,
The heaven is my throne, and the earth is my footstool: WHERE IS THE HOUSE THAT YOU BUILD UNTO ME?
AND WHERE IS THE PLACE OF MY REST?
Acts 7:49

The religious spirit will say you are not saved and do not know God if you do not "Go to church." Going to church doesn't make you any better or worse than the person who doesn't! To think so is to think so with a self-righteous spirit that turns its nose up at the man standing on the corner drinking a beer and honor the woman singing in the choir Sunday that he didn't know was sliding around the pole in the club Saturday night! However, it is the "not forsaking the assemblying" of the corporate body of believers, hearts united in praise and worship to the only one to be praised, Jesus Christ, is what draws people to Him, and not turn from Him because of self-righteousness and self-exaltation and even the more as we see the day of the Lord approaching (Hebrews 10:25).

RECOVERY FROM A CARNAL MINDSET

Great ministries are being birthed through Jesus Christ who is the Spirit of Prophecy in the 21st Century for 21st Century ministry or the testimony of Jesus is the spirit of prophecy (Revelation 19:10, KJV). The time has come to unfold a greater revelation of the truth that Christ has come to set us all free from walking the carnality of hermeneutics (the "art" of biblical interpretation through theory and practice). Romans 8:1-8 is saying to the church in the 21st Century concerning having a carnal mind:

There is therefore now no condemnation to them who are in Christ Jesus (emphasis added) who walk not after the flesh, but after the Spirit. For the law of the Spirit of life in Christ Jesus has made me free from the law of sin and death. For what the law could not do, in that it was weak through the flesh, God sending his own Son in the likeness of sinful flesh, and for sin, condemned sin in the flesh: That the righteousness of the law might be fulfilled in us, who walk not after the flesh, but after the Spirit. For they that are after the flesh do mind the things of the flesh; but they that are after the Spirit the things of the Spirit. For to be carnally minded is death; but to be spiritually minded is life and peace.
Because the carnal mind is enmity against God:
for it is not subject to the law of God, neither indeed can be.
So then they that are in the flesh cannot please God.

PROPHETIC PRONOUNCEMENT: THE CARNAL MIND IS THE SEAT OF "ENMITY" THAT GOD PUT BETWEEN THE SEED OF THE WOMAN AND THE SEED OF SATAN IN THE GARDEN.

The definition of "enmity" gives a stark contrast to the behavior of many who oppose the unique role of women in ministry as well as the men who are kept back from being used by God as well. Enmity is "the state or feeling of being actively opposed or hostile to someone or something (Easton). Enmity is further defined by Dictionary.com as "a feeling or condition of hostility; hatred; ill will; animosity; antagonism. Wow! How do you survive the adversity of the enemy exerted through by men and women "in the body of Christ" when you are carrying a seed to birth forth in your generations to birth nations?

Apostolic women who birth nations will confront false Prophets, false teachers and dethrone the seat of powers long held in the church by the Jezebel spirit. The battle for the seed is always the battle for power to rule, have dominion and to subdue. Over the years the worst spiritual attacks and spiritual wounds in the body have come from those within the body disguised as angels of light. It is the false Apostles and false Prophets that hinder the progress and advance of true kingdom ministries. Because of the hindrances and warfare set against this ministry which reforms and builds foundations, you will no doubt, at some time or another, have to confront these false Apostles and Prophets face to face because they intentionally deceive those who are not as keen in the gift of discernment. Apostles and Prophets will function in their Office with a greater capacity of discernment. Paul warns the Corinthian Church to not be surprised when they are uncovered: "And no marvel (no wonder, I am not amazed); for Satan himself is transformed into an angel of light. Therefore it is no great thing if his ministers also be transformed as the ministers of righteousness; whose end shall be according to their works" (II Corinthians 2:11-15). You will know them by their fruit.

Chapter 11:

AS SOON AS ZION TRAVAILED

Before she travailed, she brought forth; before her pain came,
she was delivered of a man child. Who hath heard such a thing?
Who hath seen such things?
Shall the earth be made to bring forth in one day?
OR SHALL A NATION BE BORN AT ONCE?
For as soon as Zion travailed, she brought forth her children.
Shall I bring to the birth, and not cause to bring forth? saith the LORD: shall I cause to bring forth, and shut the womb? saith thy God.
Isaiah 66:8-9

Reformation, recovery and restoration from the issues that are affecting the nation, the church, and have inflicted spiritual wounds in the Body of Christ, have reached the peak of travail. Travail defined means "pain, anguish or suffering resulting from mental or physical hardship." I believe we are in a time when as the Prophet Isaiah speaks to us of the audacity and improbability of God bringing forth this emerging new wineskin. He sees as we are seeing the prophecy fulfilled in the 21st a nation that will come forth at once – as soon as Zion travails! He begins by looking backward and saying before the pain of the issues, problems, politics, religious dogma, gender strife, the abuse, wars and rumors of wars Isaiah says before the pain came, she brought forth a Son. Not just a son but a full and mature Son. It is the sound and cry of the whole earth that groans waiting to see the manifestation of the Sons of God!

"For the earnest expectation of the creation
waits for the manifestation of the Sons of God.
For the creation was made subject to vanity, not willingly,
but by reason of him who has subjected the same in hope,
Because the creation itself also shall be delivered from the bondage
of corruption into the glorious liberty of the children of God.
For we know that the whole creation groans and travails in pain
together
"UNTIL NOW"
Romans 8:19-22

To answer the birth pangs of all creation and silence the Prophet's inquiry, God answers the Prophet Jeremiah. *"Before I formed thee in the belly I knew thee; and before thou camest forth out of the womb I sanctified thee, and I ordained thee a Prophet unto the nations (Jeremiah 1:5, KJV).* God has already caused this birthing of nations to come forth. He sees the end from the beginning. *I am the Alpha (the beginning) and the Omega (the end) and I started this process and purpose of the seed to come forth from the womb.*

Nothing happened until Zion travailed. We have been silent too long by our own philosophies and mindsets that have given us a narrow view of the purpose and original intent of

God for the Church and the pursuit of life, liberty and justice for all. God will move when we move in His divine timing against our traditions, gender strife, as we take up our cross and follow Him. Our role as God's gifts should extend beyond the four walls of the church to address the issues and challenges facing our nation today. When we begin to travail in the spirit in prayer to birth healing to the nations, the Body of Christ will come into divine order to bring forth God's intent even against the enemy's attempts to stop it as soon as Zion travails.

God will especially move when the enemy is set so high to steal, kill and to destroy what He created in you to produce. God's hand is there to protect the seed and He understands the language of the cry that is upon the nation. Any ministry that is set to birth a nation will experience multiple and intense labor pains that releases this cry of travail in Zion. If you are called to the five-fold ministry and you have never experienced the type of intense warfare and the need to travail in prayer for the issues facing the nation perhaps you should take a Gifts Test Analysis and find that you are not really called to the five-fold ministry but you should be teaching children's church or working with the Media Ministry assisting with the multi-media presentations. Spiritual Travail is a level of intensity marked by a burden of prayer, praise and prophecy to actually bring to pass a given promise, a Prophetic insight or a person, church, city or nation. The cry of travail when it reaches its peak in contractions will bring forth what you have carried and labored to deliver. There is a set time to be delivered to deliver the nation and that is the time that God hears the cry of travail in the womb of the Spirit to PULL you through to your destiny. Jesus became a curse to destroy the curse in the garden of our genesis, but the travail that causes multiplied birth pangs, contractions to give birth will become so intense that God will move when it's heard in Zion by the daughters of Zion!

"For I have heard a voice as of a woman in travail,
and the anguish as of her that bringeth forth her first child,
the voice of the daughter of Zion,
that bewaileth herself, that spreadeth her hands, saying,
Woe is me now! for my soul is wearied
because of murderers!"
Isaiah 61:3

For Zion's sake will I not hold my peace, and for Jerusalem's sake
I will not rest, until the righteousness thereof go forth as brightness,
and the salvation thereof as a lamp that burneth
Isaiah 62:1

Part Three

THE BIRTH PANGS OF RESTORATION

Chapter 12:

THE SECOND COMING OF APOSTOLIC BOLDNESS

Restoration is the bringing of something back to its original design and intent. In the times of restoration that we are experiencing in the 21st Century we can see the fulfillment of many thought provocative scriptures that is shifting mindsets for the birthing of an Apostolic and Prophetic nation and advancing the Kingdom of God. The process of reformation and restoration requires a shifting of mindsets and a MOVEMENT which has always been difficult because we fear change. Yet change is necessary and is always met with resistance by the attempted use of force through threats of loss, or imposed by Government sanctions when dealing with other nations; in this case "a chosen generation, a royal priesthood, an holy nation, a peculiar people" (I Peter 2:9, KJV).

The Protestant Reformation to reform the Catholic Church in Western Europe began in 1517 by a German monk named Martin Luther. It was a time to shift the corruption and practices he saw within the Church. Martin Luther decided to take authority and exercise boldness to bring down a spirit of religion and deception in his day and time by nailing ninety-five theses to a door! I am sure his writings were inspired by hearing the voice of God to bring revelation to release people from religious bondage and give them the truth about forgiveness of sin through faith in Jesus Christ, not by paying condolences. It upset the "systems" so much that it led to revolt and a thirty year war in Europe between 1618 and 1648 between major European powers. The war of powers against religious institutional systems spiritual wickedness in high places is not a war that is easily won overnight. Boldness is necessary but patience is necessary too in the 21st Century. The result of the war of powers initiated by Martin Luther resulted in the domination of Protestantism in parts of Germany, Switzerland, Scandinavia, England and Scotland (citing in part from Wikipedia).

The ministry for the 21st Century that you are carrying to birth nations is a part of a great Kingdom movement that will grow and cannot be stopped even if you want it to. Paul said he despaired of life itself because of the persecution and suffering that it took in to order to birth nations into the Kingdom of God. This is a ministry that the chief priests, religious rulers and ranking heads of power are fighting to resist to keep others from ever coming into the knowledge of the truth that is revealed through Apostolic and Prophetic new wineskins.

The Book of Acts is unfolding in a dynamic way in our time as we are witnessing a time when even the mention of Jesus' name in public places is met with the spirit of offense and demands of tolerance of other gods eroding the foundation of America as a Christian nation. How we allowed these imposed threats and sanctions to change the authority - to dominate the authority that Christ gave the church to subdue kingdoms is a question that this generation will have to answer. By re-discovering and re-examining our indoctrinated beliefs to release the sound of revelational truth with bold declarations and confessions of our faith as did the Apostles in the Book of Acts – we can turn this thing around!

They turned cities upside down by the authority given them by Jesus Christ with apostolic boldness empowered by the Holy Spirit that should be in effect in the 21st Century for a time such as this:

"Now when the high priest and the captain of the temple and the chief priests heard these things, they doubted of them whereunto this would grow. Then came one and told them, saying, Behold, the men whom ye put in prison are standing in the temple, and teaching the people. Then went the captain with the officers, and brought them without violence: for they feared the people, lest they should have been stoned. And when they had brought them, they set them before the council: and the high priest asked them, Saying, Did not we straitly command you that ye should not teach in this name? and, behold, ye have filled Jerusalem with your doctrine, and intend to bring this man's blood upon us. Then Peter and the other Apostles answered and said, We ought to obey God rather than men. The God of our fathers raised up Jesus, whom ye slew and hanged on a tree. Him hath God exalted with his right hand to be a Prince and a Saviour, for to give repentance to Israel, and forgiveness of sins. And we are his

witnesses of these things; and so is also the Holy Ghost, whom God hath given to them that obey him"
Acts 5:24-32, KJV

To hear God is to obey God by moving in the power of the Holy Spirit. We are in a time where nothing will stop the move of God! It does not matter whether how long traditional and religious beliefs have been held to deny the Apostolic and Prophetic calling that is on the Sons of God from coming forth – it cannot be stopped! The apostolic authority and overshadowing power of the Holy Ghost that was upon the first birth of the Christ and the Church that fell upon the disciples in the upper room and baptized them with fire then is still upon the BELIEVERS today – like it or not! Agree with it or not! Nothing will stop the emergence of this Prophetic birthing of nations to advance the Kingdom in the 21st Century.

Apostolic authority is given as "signs and wonders" and produces miracles to take place in your life and those that your sphere of influence "sends" you to. Every one of you are carriers to release the sound of heaven and SHIFT the position (mindsets, false beliefs and lower levels of thinking) of what is hidden as treasure in these earthen vessels. The power and authority being released to the nations is the excellency that IS OF GOD – not of man, II Corinthians 4:7: *But WE have this treasure in earthen vessels, that the excellency of the power may be of God, and not of us.*

When we look at our lives and embrace this call to move into the realm of the Apostolic and Prophetic, reading this scripture presents an oxymoron to the religious teaching by leaders who set their own standards and qualifications of who is and who is not called to preach, teach and minister the gospel. This treasure that we have is not by gender qualification taken of one verse of scripture taken totally out of context: Galatians 3:22-28 applies to the Body of Christ, the church corporately, both male and female and all who name the name of Jesus Christ and are called according to His purpose:

"But before faith came, WE were kept under the law, shut up unto the faith which should afterwards be revealed. Wherefore the law was our schoolmaster to bring us unto Christ, that WE might be justified by faith. But after that faith is come, WE are no longer under a schoolmaster."

For ye are all the children of God by faith in Christ Jesus. For as many of you as have been baptized into Christ have put on Christ. There is neither Jew nor Greek, there is neither bond nor free, there is neither male nor female: for ye are all one in Christ Jesus."

WE are troubled on every side, yet not distressed; WE are perplexed, but not in despair; Persecuted, but not forsaken; cast down, but not destroyed; Always bearing about in the body the dying of the Lord Jesus, that the life also of Jesus might be made manifest in our body. For WE which live are always delivered unto death for Jesus' sake, that the life also of Jesus might be made manifest in our mortal flesh.

So then death worketh in us, but life in you.

If WE experience the same things Paul experienced for the cause, we can't help but to speak in His name!

But Peter and John answered and said unto them, Whether it be right in the sight of God to hearken unto you more than unto God, judge you. For we cannot but speak the things which we have seen and heard. So when they had further threatened them, they let them go, finding nothing for which they might punish them, because of the people: for all men glorified God for that which was done.
Acts 4:20-21, KJV

THE DANGER OF DOUBT AND UNBELIEF

Just as there are many who doubt today the Second Coming of Christ, it is really frightening to see how many of the "chief priests" today are doubting and not even preaching His Second Coming anymore. Eschatology has been replaced by "self-help" sermons. Paul before the High Priest, the captains of the temple and the chief priest DOUBTED that this KINGDOM MOVEMENT would grow. There are many doubters today that are posting all over the internet denying that the sound of the Kingdom through the voices of Apostles and Prophets will grow and that it will die out. Many believe things will just remain the same and God is in some far off distant place just letting things continue as they are. The religious rulers and the Pharisees did everything they could to silence this Apostolic and Prophetic voice that was emerging and coming forth to CRUSH THE HEAD of their religious structures and systems and breaking their traditional stronghold that denied the people the right to worship God in Spirit and in truth. Men, and some women under the influence of this false teaching, are still denying the overshadowing power of the Holy Ghost that has anointed men and especially WOMEN to walk in their calling as Apostles and Prophets. "They" doubt say and teach that women are not called to be in the Office as an Apostle or Prophet. They say that the Office of Apostle was done away with. They say that women have no business pastoring a Church. They say that women ought to be silent in the Church.

Religious thinkers (rulers) and theologians have placed the emphasis on the gender of the one being sent and not according to Rightmire on the one who sends.

> "It is evident that the Apostles formed the nucleus of primitive Christianity. The New Testament highlights their function as Apostles, without delineating in detail the authoritative nature of their Office in relation to the Church. What is emphasized is that their apostolic commission authorized them to preach (1 Corinthians 1:17); to be ambassadors for Christ (2 Corinthians 5:20; Ephesians 6:20); to be witnesses to all nations (Luke 24:48); and to

make disciples of all peoples (Matthew 28:19)" (Rightmire).

An Apostle (Greek, Apostolo) is defined as an envoy, ambassador, or messenger commissioned to carry out the instructions of the commissioning agent. Thus, the Septuagint uses the apostello [ajpostevllw] word-group to denote the authorization of an individual to fulfill a particular function, with emphasis on the one who sends, not on the one who is sent. In the New Testament apostolos is applied to Jesus as the Sent One of God (Hebrew 3:1), to those sent by God to preach to Israel (Luke 11:49), to those sent by Churches (2 Colossians 8:23 ; Philippians 2:25), and most often, to the individuals who had been appointed by Christ to preach the gospel of the kingdom.

This latter category, however, is understood differently by New Testament writers. For example, Luke-Acts uses the term "apostle" to refer almost exclusively to the Twelve, while Paul uses it in relation to a broader group of individuals. The expression "all the Apostles" in 1 Corinthians 15:7 seems to include more than the twelve referred to in verse 5. James is considered here, and in Galatians 1:19, to be an apostle. Barnabas is referred to as an apostle in Acts 14:14 (11:22-24 ; 13:1-4). Paul calls Andronicus and Junias Apostles in Romans 16:7. Paul's own claim to Apostleship is likewise BASED ON THE DIVINE CALL OF CHRIST (Rom 1:1 ; 1 Col 1:1 ;Galatians 1:1 Galatians 1:15; cf. 2 Col 1:1; Eph 1:1 ; Col 1:1 ; 1 Tim 1:1 ; 2 Tim

1:1; Titus 1:1). He is an apostle, "not from men nor by man, but by Jesus Christ and God the Father, who raised him from the dead" (Gal 1:1).

THE BOOK OF ACTS IS IN EFFECT

It is time for those who are in denial to break away from the old, traditional, long held false beliefs that your interpretation of Scripture is supreme over the REVELATION of the truth. It is time to bow down and worship Him, enter into the Kingdom! It is time to repent and submit to the Lordship of Jesus Christ. The walls of religion, the wicked deception and spiritual abuse by leaders is over. The Apostolic and Prophetic new wineskins cannot be kept imprisoned behind the walls of institutional thinkers. Reformation for kingdom advance is here and the truth is, *you cannot stop it!*

"Behold, the men whom ye put in prison
Are standing in the temple,
And teaching the people"
Acts 5:25

Take a look around the nation and see that the ones you said had no right to preach and teach in the Church are STANDING IN THE TEMPLE! The ones that you thought were dead in the lion's den have stood up in the fire for years for the times of restoration, recovery and reformation that is upon the nations today. Not only standing up but running with the vision for the years religion has controlled and limited the freedom of the Holy Spirit to MOVE in the sanctuary. The Ministers and Gifts of God that the Jezebelic Prophets and abusive leaders from the corporate boardroom to the church Board of Directors who tried to drive God's called and chosen insane by their witchcrafts and sorceries are running corporations and positioning themselves for the greatest transfer of the wealth of the wicked from a man that robbed God. The ones you PUT IN PRISON, and had bound by your traditions and religious strongholds are doing everything they said they could not do. Why? Apostolic authority negates rules and restrictions of man and supersedes religious authority with Spiritual Authority!

"Did not we straitly command you
That ye should not teach in this name?
And, behold, ye have filled Jerusalem with your doctrine,
And intend to bring this man's blood upon us.

Then Peter and the other apostles answered and said,
We ought to obey God rather than men!"
Acts 5:28-29

Chapter 13:

THE RESTORATION OF TRUE APOSTOLIC FATHERS AND SPIRITUAL MOTHERS FOR THE 21ST CENTURY CHURCH

As noted earlier, Apostolic Fathers were students of the Apostles where the principle of prophecy fulfillment was used as a "Divine Approach" to bible interpretation. Over the last three years God has blessed me with wise, mature spiritual mothers and fathers who have breathed into my soul to help me get up again and walk in the fullness of my calling as an Apostle breaking all of my glass ceilings. A True Apostolic Father and Spiritual Mother will push you out of the nest when you think you are not ready to fly. Like an eagle, instinctively by Prophetic revelation they know it's your time to move from a position of pushing others to a place of leading others. They don't hold you back. They stand you up, hold your hand, then let you go so that you can walk on your own. They know there are nations waiting to hear your voice, to heal the soul of a nation that has been spiritually wounded, dropped, broken, that is about to lose their mind like you were! The power of resurrection that came for you is the same resurrection power you will take to the nations. Because their hearts have been turned towards God's love for His children, their heart is to see to it that you go further and do better than they did in their generation. That's a Spiritual Mother. That's a true Apostolic Father.

The restoration of true Apostolic Fathers and Spiritual Mothers will bless and not curse their children. They will rally your support and will not be intimidated by your calling or feel threatened by your anointing. It is a shame that the mothers both in the natural and spiritual in this generation are jealous of their daughter's beauty, talents and the glory of the Lord that radiates through their ministries.

I have three spiritual mothers who possess "mother-wit" that spiritual fathers cannot give me. There are degrees of wisdom that a son can only get from a father. Spiritual fathers don't commit spiritual adultery by sleeping with the sheep and they do not rape the sheep! I attended a church where the Bishop was so controlling and had the people so in fear and threatened them saying he was going to break the sheep's legs! Spiritual fathers take care of the sheep. Spiritual fathers do not rob the sheep in tithes and offerings!

Shall I not punish for these things? Says the lord:
And shall not my soul be avenged on such a nation as this?
Go you up upon her walls, and destroy; but make not a full end:
Take away her branches; for they are not the Lord's.
Jeremiah 5:9-10

God is visiting the fatherless because of the generations of abuse by spiritual leaders. Worldwide outreach ministries are being birthed by women that God called and "sent" by an apostolic commissioning to bring relief, food, clothing, food and build shelters for millions of widows and homeless children worldwide. Apostolic Women who are birthing nations are glad to share their network of resources and the influence they are given to help further the work of the ministry without feeling threatened or intimidated with the fear that "they will get further ahead of me." These women have the anointing to draw thousands to hear the preaching of the gospel and to motivate groups to achieve the common goal of advancing, not hindering or frustrating, the rebuilding of the walls. Everybody who is called to the work of the ministry is called to rebuild the wall beyond the four walls, to build up the old waste places, to raise the foundation of many generations, repair the generational breach between, especially during 1980 and 2013, and to restore the paths of God to dwell in the garden of our genesis. Recovery and restoration from the routine traditional, religious "programming," everyone with his hands (all five-fold, male and female, sons and daughters) has an apostolic hammer in one hand and a Prophetic intercessor's anointing in the other!

"They which builded on the wall, and they that bare burdens, with those that laded,
Every one with one of his hands wrought in the work, and with the other hand held a weapon"

Nehemiah 4:17

"Hear, O our God; for we are despised: and turn their reproach upon their own head, and give them for a prey in the land of captivity: And cover not their iniquity, and let not their sin be blotted out from before thee: for they have provoked thee to anger before the builders. So built we the wall; and all the wall was joined together unto the half thereof:
FOR THE PEOPLE HAD A MIND TO WORK"
Nehemiah 4:4-7

PROPHETIC PRONOUNCEMENT: THE DAY IS OVER THAT THE RELIGIOUS SPIRIT AND FALSE TEACHING OF WOMEN BEING SILENT IN THE CHURCH AND SPIRITUAL ABUSE OF LEADERS BOTH FOREIGN AND DOMESTIC IS OVER! APOSTOLIC WOMEN BIRTHING NATIONS HAVE LEFT THE BUILDING OF PREACHING "ON THE ROSTER" OR BEING "ON THE PROGRAM" TO PROPHESYING AND SPEAKING TO NATIONS THROUGH BLOG TALK RADIO, SOCIAL MEDIA NETWORKS, CONFERENCE CALLS, PRAYER LINES, DIRECTING PLAYS, WRITING BOOKS, BEING INTERVIEWED NOT ONLY ON CHRISTIAN RADIO AND TELEVISION NETWORKS, BUT ALSO IN CORPORATE BOARD ROOMS, BUSINESS NETWORKING SEMINARS, AND GOING INTO ALL THE WORLD TO PREACH THE GOSPEL. IT

> WOULD BE PRAISEWORTHY TO SURVEY THE NUMBER OF MISSIONARY TRIPS THAT HAVE BEEN AND ARE BEING SPEARHEADED BY WOMEN WHO GOD HAS ORDAINED AS APOSTLES IN THE 21ST CENTURY. TO BE SILENT NOW IS TO REMAIN SILENT FOREVER WITH SO MANY "OPEN DOORS AND OPEN HEAVENS" THAT GOD HAS PROVIDED.

The 21st Century God has opened doors and placed mantles upon those who will lift up their voice like a trumpet restored to having a Kingdom mindsets to birth nations. Their apostolic boldness is not concerned that they upset the religious order. For that they praise God like Paul saying, "And I thank Christ Jesus our Lord, who has enabled me, that he counted me faithful, putting me into the ministry" (I Timothy 1:12, KJV). I am excited about it, breaking down again the walls of partition and tearing down the veil of the temple that religion, tradition and false gods that have separated us!

NOBODY CAN STOP IT – LET THEM GO!

That's what happened in the book of Luke when the praise of God became so loud and the voice of the Apostles RELEASED THE SOUND of the Kingdom that the religious rulers and elders told Jesus to make them be quiet. We usually ask "what would Jesus do" but I want to ask you "what did Jesus say?" His response to the religious status quo, legalistic abiding

Pharisees and religious ruling "church folk" should be the believer's response in the 21st Century: "If these should hold their peace, the rocks would cry out." But the stony hearted antagonist theologians would rationalize and argue that rocks do not have the human capacity to "cry out" and we don't have to be so emotional! The enemy touched my mind, God raised me from the dead – YOU CAN'T STOP IT.

And now I say unto you, refrain from these men,
And let them alone:
For if this counsel or this work be of men,
it will come to nothing:
But if it be of God, you cannot overthrow it;
Lest perhaps you be found even to fight against God.
And to him they agreed: and when they had called the apostles, and beaten them, they commanded that they should not speak in the name of Jesus,
And let them go.
Acts 5:28-40

PROPHETIC PRONOUNCEMENT: THE DAYS OF THE SANBALAT AND TOBIAS SPIRIT ARE OVER!

A Kingdom mindset is a TEAM (together everyone achieves more) model for ministry mindset, one for all and all for one. It does not care who gets the credit, they just do the work. They are not concerned about "how much money" they will make but how many lives will be changed by what they do

- That's apostolic! As a woman in ministry, you have to know and understand that you have been given a distinct ability to birth nations through your womb, naturally and spiritually! The man's role is to plant the seed but only a woman can give birth! The curse was broken when the man did not protect, nurture and defend the seed so God planted a supernatural seed by the Holy Ghost and the woman conceived and brought forth a Son – Jesus Christ, the Son of the Living God through 42 generations crushing the enemy's head!

However long it takes to do what God called you to do, do not allow any of the distractions, attacks, or multiplied sorrows to keep you from birthing the multiple anointings and giftings that you are carrying for your generations.

SPIRITUAL COVERING EMPOWERED BY THE PROPHETIC

True spiritual covering is taking on a greater dimension as we embrace a shift of attitudes towards gender qualifications and recognizing the anointing that is birthing nations into greater revelation, reformation, recovery and restoration of our identity as Kingdom citizens and joint heirs with Christ. If you have suffered with Him you are positioned to reign with Him. 2013 is the year of Restoration! The close of the Old Testament and the silent years between the New Testament where there was no Prophetic voice heard, there is a cry in the nation in the 21st Century that is releasing the sound and heartbeat of God as He closes with the last verse in

Malachi, Chapter 4 that *"Behold I will send you Elijah the Prophet before the coming of the great and dreadful day of the Lord: And he shall turn the heart of the fathers to the children, and the children to their fathers, lest I come and smite the earth with a curse!"*

A great awakening is upon the nations as the identity of what is meant to be a spiritual mother or father to sons and daughters who are growing up in ministry in a time where the world is turning upside down and inside out. The raising of sons and daughters for the Kingdom will turn it right side up. The spiritual abuse by leaders who did not, and many today still do not, understand their role in the natural and spiritual as being fathers. I believe there are true Spiritual Mothers and Apostolic Fathers who have taken up the call to raise up spiritual sons and daughters who understand their apostolic mandate concerning the seed that will again crush the head of the enemy by helping and not hindering one another in the birthing process. It's time to Celebrate the our Recovery and Prepare for the Full Restoration of Apostolic Fathers and Spiritual Mothers!

CELEBRATION OF LEGACY HONORING SPIRITUAL MOTHERS

The hearts of the fathers are being turned to the children, and the heart of the children to their fathers. Spiritual fathering and spiritual mothers are being restored in the house of God who will as the Prophet Isaiah points to the

21st Century generation of leaders that would build up the old waste places who have shifted from a church mentality to a kingdom mentality and will RAISE THE FOUNDATION!

"And they that shall be of thee shall build the old waste places: thou shalt RAISE UP THE FOUNDATIONS of many generations; and thou shalt be called, The repairer of the breach, The restorer of paths to dwell in"
Isaiah 58:12

FROM CONCEPTION TO DELIVERY!

"A woman when she is in travail hath sorrow, because her hour is come: but as soon as she is delivered of the child, she remembereth no more the anguish, for joy that a man is born into the world. And ye now therefore have sorrow:
but I will see you again, and your heart shall rejoice,
AND YOUR JOY NO MAN TAKETH FROM YOU"
John 16:21-22

When God restores what the enemy tears down, He restores it bigger better and stronger than it was before! I created a "Kingdom Talk Show" that God started at FPM while I was in the conference center. God reminded me through my Assistant Pastors Lang and Joan Mason, "that you were born for this. God prepared you when we were at the conference center to do a talk show, don't you remember?" I had forgotten about the vision. I wept and I cried and praised God for the restoration of what He had spoken then that it is coming to pass now! It has been three years since I had to cancel my lease at the conference center and I put everything in a box and put a lid on it. I cried every time I saw my posters of Fully Persuaded Ministries that showed the date and location. It was like the vision had died and all I could do was get into a place to be healed in my mind or else I would lose it.

Just before the Prophetic Flow Conference I was blessed to be a part of here in Houston. I was assigned to open the conference with prayer before Dr. Juanita Bynum brought the message. The day before the conference I was given an opportunity to do a LIVE TV taping on THE WORD NETWORK! It was my "due date" to deliver to the nations the sound of Fully Persuaded Ministries, announce the release of this book, and talk about the vision God gave me to establish a "Celebration of Legacy Luncheon Honoring Spiritual Mothers" for the purpose of passing the mantles of God's apostolic women who have been generals, pioneers, trailblazers and forerunners who blazed the path for many sons and daughters to mentor, train, equip, labor in prayer for their ministries and churches to come forth! I released that it was time for those sons and daughters to rise up and call them blessed! It was also for the sons and daughters in this generation that were coming forth in ministry to receive an impartation from the Honorees anointing to carry from one generation to the next. As I considered the time we are in for 21st Century ministry and birthing the Apostolic and Prophetic nation, God named it: "RAISING THE FOUNDATION" (Isaiah 58:12). He said that even upon the ministry of the arts and dance He was going to raise the foundation for the Prophetic in dance and worship. So He gave Pastor Adrienne Rowe and Minister Stacey Johnson to be Honorees in the 2013 Legacy Luncheon. I am completing this book before the "due date!"

"The Kingdom of heaven is like unto a certain king, which made a marriage for his son, So those servants went out into the highways, and gathered together all as many as they found, both bad and good: and the wedding was furnished with guests."
Matthew 22:2, 10, KJV

Even with the anointing of the birth pangs I felt when He spoke this assignment, I was so nervous and afraid to call THE WORD NETWORK to set the appointment because it was bigger than what I felt I could carry and deliver. I tried to give the opportunity to my son, Prophet Richard Harper and to my

General Commander Pastor Cassandra Scott, but they pushed it back to me saying they weren't available! One of my spiritual mothers, Mother Holley, said that I better go on out there and do it. She said that God always gives me something and I always try to give it away trying to help somebody else. She threatened to whip me with a mango stick. I had never seen a mango stick but it sounded scary so I told her I would go on and do it! I was even afraid to call the Producer back to set the appointment.

When God gives you an assignment it's bigger than you and will cause you to tremble. I had two days to make a decision. Then I remembered the words of Bishop T.D. Jakes in his book, "God's Leading Ladies" (The Potters Shelf, p. 19):

> *"This analogy of preparing to take your place onstage applies to you RIGHT NOW even as you are reading (I read this book over eight years ago!). It is a call to action to prepare us for greater and greater opportunities if we are willing to trust Him and His TIMING for our lives. We must be willing to accept the leading role God has scripted just for us. We must be willing to transform our "acting" into an authentic performance that unleashes who we really are. Your strength is in your struggle and your power is in your pain."*

Then God said, "You have to go. This is your first interview. You have to get used to the cameras and the set and understand how television taping works and the business side of it." I returned the call and set the appointment.

If I failed to let go of everything else including my fears and busyness working for the church, I would not have been in the RIGHT POSITION to bear down and push this book out. If I gave in to my fears of doing the LIVE TV taping with The Word Network on Saturday at noon, and being so committed to helping someone else with their conference on Friday, I would not have been prepared to step into a new level that God had SET before me.

After assisting with the Prophetic Flow Ministries conference that Thursday night before the set time, I was to be on the set with The Word Network. Understand that the doors God will open for you will open doors for many others. As an apostolic ministry you are sent first (proton) to blaze a path for others to follow. In this season you will learn to keep time with God beyond time even if it means breaking commitments or anything else that you are carrying that has been holding you back.

PROPHETIC PRONOUNCEMENT: I DECREE AND I DECLARE THAT WOMEN ARE BREAKING THEIR POTS IN THIS 21ST CENTURY AND RUNNING WITH LIVING WATER TO BIRTH NATIONS WHOSE WELLS WILL NEVER RUN DRY!

Chapter 14:

RESTORATION OF APOSTOLIC AND PROPHETIC INTERCESSION FOR 21ST CENTURY MINISTRY

The power of Apostolic Fathers and Spiritual Mothers in this time of reformation, recovery and restoration will have to confront the sin of our forefathers that is over the nations. That's the type and shadow of the seed that will crush the head of the enemy that is seated by principalities and powers and spiritual wickedness in high places. Our nation's foundations have again been cracked by the sin of sexual perversion and God is coming down to see about it.

"Because the cry of Sodom and Gomorrah is great, and because their sin is very grievous I will go down now, and see whether they have done altogether according to the cry of it, which is come unto me; and if not, I will know. And the men turned their faces from thence, and went toward Sodom:
BUT ABRAHAM STOOD YET BEFORE THE LORD."
Gen. 18:20

There has come a time when even the traditional religious spirit in men will not let the men or women keep silent. When there is an emergency need for God to move for us like never before the cry goes out, "We need to have a prayer meeting, we need a revival, God save us!" Nobody will challenge the authority of anyone who has the audacity to hope and cry loud and spare not. Nobody has cried loud enough about women being silent in the church, about the sexual pervasion, about the rich getting richer, the poor getting poorer, the bigotry and bullying in our schools.

Prophetic intercession stands between heaven and earth as Abraham did before the Lord to not only birth a nation but to save a nation. This type and shadow of intercession saves nations and births revivals that are needed for recovery and restoration to repair the breach and restore the paths to dwell in. Abraham prayed and interceded before God to save the City of Sodom and Gomorrah started by asking God if you find 50 and went down deeper into Prophetic intercession asking God please don't be angry at all of us, and he kept on interceding saying, "Lord if you find just 10 righteous men in will you spare the City until God said,

"I will not destroy it for ten's sake.
And the LORD went his way, as soon as he had left communing with Abraham: and Abraham returned unto his place"
Genesis 18:22-33

The hand of the Lord is upon this 21st Century ready to execute judgment. Although our President Barak Obama has said that the people have the right to marry whoever they have chosen to marry and to love whomever they have chosen to love. I have contended at the gate that he is right – they do.

Our nation and Constitution is built upon a system of rights and restrictions and punishments for violation of rights, duties and responsibilities. God has a system too that punishes sin for disobedience and violation of His Holy Statutes and breaking of His Spiritual Covenants. HOWEVER, God is RAISING THE FOUNDATION and the standard of freedom of choice. There is a remnant Joshua Generation emerging who are crying loud and sparing not declaring:

Now therefore fear the LORD, and serve him in sincerity and in truth: and put away the gods which your fathers served on the other side of the flood, and in Egypt; and serve ye the LORD. And if it seem evil unto you to serve the LORD, CHOOSE YOU THIS DAY WHOM YE WILL SERVE; whether the gods which your fathers served that were on the other side of the flood, or the gods of the Amorites, in whose land ye dwell: BUT AS FOR ME AND MY HOUSE, WE WILL SERVE THE LORD
Joshua 24:14-15

COMMISSIONED BY THE SPIRIT

Apostles are being sent into regions across the nation to rebuild the old waste places that have been devastated by drugs, gang violence, and a decline in prayer. When you walk in the Office as an Apostle, covered, submitted and governed by an Apostolic Alliance and Network of Apostolic Spiritual Fathers and Spiritual Mothers, spiritual authority is extended to you by protocol, by rank and by order of spiritual authority as commissioned by the Spirit. Authority is given and is always subject to a higher ranking authority as ordained by God (Romans 8:13). Apostles do not just have a "title" they FUNCTION in an Office as a Delegated Kingdom Ambassador.

REVIVING A CITY-REBUILDING THE OLD WASTE PLACES

A few years ago God began to reveal His plan that Revival was about to hit the Midwest Region. He sent me to my hometown in South Bend, Indiana, a place where the foundation of the prayers of our generation's forefathers, of spiritual mothers and elders, through pastors like Elder Willie Coates at Emmanuel Temple (the Pastor on my father's side) and Rev. Charles G. Rowlett our family Pastor at Pilgrim Baptist Church (the Pastor on my mother's side) had been cracked. God showed me that there was a breach between our generations and the sons and daughters had grown up and were coming home to rebuild the walls that had been torn down. There is a call in the 21st Century to repair the breach of generations. All of my life I have remembered that it was power of the sincere, heartfelt prayers of my generation's preachers, fathers, mothers, intercessors that kept the watch over the City and kept the order in the house that were now in a breached position between ten years having no strong leaders to stand in the gap between the generations. After I arrived at the airport and as I drove around the City I heard the sound of desolation and the Spirit said, "The foundations have been cracked! This is an excerpt from the message I preached at New Philadelphia Church Ministries given an open door by

Pastors Willie & Ruth Moore in South Bend, Indiana, May, 2011:

"THE FOUNDATION OF THE CHURCH WAS CRACKED"

- When the "pulpit" was torn down and what was built was a "platform" and the spirit of entertainment to appease the flesh that did nothing for the soul.

- When the mothers of the Church either passed on to glory or were pushed aside. In the 21st Century, the mothers of the church women are no longer in position on the foundation and the young women are without the role model of a godly mother who would when I was coming up would check you at the door and demand a right attitude of respect, we couldn't even chew gum and your dress better be below you knee, if your slip was hanging they'd let you know they wouldn't allow you to wear anything that might be seductive.

- When our posture of humility shifted at the altar shifted from coming to the altar on bended knees in holy fear and reverence for the Lord prostrate and helpless because we knew we really needed Him

- When we went from a sincere trembling before His holy presence to dancing in the flesh

- When we shifted from our knees in prayer to standing up in arrogance and pride because God had blessed us so much we became spoiled and took on a "expect a miracle" blessing just because you're so wonderful.
- When we started driving better, looking better, doing better, and so now they no longer bowed down to worship
- Then the foundations became cracked when in the 90s everybody was told "oh you don't have to do all that after all God loves you and He said come as you are. And they did and nobody did or said anything when satan came too, going up and down in it seeking whom he may devour. Then the Jezebel spirit came, manipulation in giving, witches and warlocks, false Prophets and teachers, heresy – they all came too. . People came just as they are and left the same way because the foundation was cracked - no standard, come half naked, don't dress up at all no standard just come. Mother Boards we don't need y'all, deacons we don't need y'all. But then the worst crack in the foundation came when the Pastors took off the collars, took off the robes and put on flashy three piece Armani suits and alligator shoes, took off the title of Pastor because they got the M. Div and the PhD and psychologically convinced themselves

that are they are beyond themselves because they learned a few words in Greek and Hebrew, puffed up with hermeneutics and homiletics and the people began to worship them as gods! Idolatry was rampant and demanded that the people bow down to worship them. All the while God was saying, "And they throw money on my altar gambling, placing a wager on my Word - Shall I not visit them for these things saith the Lord! If it has been your way of showing appreciation for the word of God "to put money on It" when you hear a word, you cannot bet on the Word.

- The foundation was not only cracked but when the moral fabric of our society began to erode away the walls of the Church standing as a moral influence in the nation and the people began to cast off all restraint. During the 20th Century between the years 1985 through 1995 gang violence erupted from the east side to the westside to the south side to the north side. During the decade between1995 to 2005 the foundation was then split and split families across the nation when crack cocaine became epidemic, HIV / Aids had become an epidemic and marriages began to unravel and is "judicially" by political voting power being redefined. Today, more marriages are ending in divorce by people who "go to church."

- For years nothing was done to repair the huge crack in the nation's education foundation when a known atheist by the name of Madeline O'Hare manipulated her ungodly propaganda to influence legislation through our judicial system to take prayer out of schools. This nation is still being led by a dead woman's bad and ungodly idea and we are still under the control of this antichrist spirit.

"The only way to kill a bad idea is to replace it with a good idea"
Dr. Myles Munroe

Chapter 15:

KINGDOM KIN-NECTIONS FOR KINGDOM ASSIGNMENTS

A RESTORER OF PATHS TO DWELL IN

In order for some things to move, a voice has to speak. "Imagine the power of one voice" is a commercial that always captures my attention. There is a SOUND to the true voices of Apostles and Prophets that gets everybody's attention. I was invited by my friend Dorothy to a prayer line where that sound of apostolic women birth nations was being released and the midwives were helping to birth ministries under the leadership of Dr. Cassandra Scott, Pastor of Turning Point Faith Ministries in Houston, Texas. I had heard of her but I had never met nor heard her preach but I was sure hearing her now! It was six months after I had to relinquish my lease at the conference center and close the doors to Fully Persuaded Ministries worship services. That was the hardest thing for me to do but I had to do it in order to recover and not lose my mind. During my rehabilitation, recovery and restoration process God was healing my mind, body, soul and reviving my spirit. For months I had been hiding from public engagements or attending conferences afraid someone would invite to pulpit to "have some words" or to pray. I didn't want anybody to see me because I felt so ashamed that the ministry and the beautiful place that I had told everybody that God gave me to start the ministry was closed. I could hear the haters who told me that it wasn't going to work because I didn't have a husband covering me. I was really afraid to get close to anyone after a "friend" introduced me to a wolf then joined in his attempt to destroy me. This wolf in sheep's clothing deceived the minds of the people distorting my image, deviling my character, sabotaging my ministry and saying that I was a witch and had a Jezebel spirit! Many connected to that camp have told you one side of the story. But there are always two sides to every story, now you know mine.

Moreover, Pastors who were my "friends" who I had served and helped to build their churches told me that while others were saying God did not call women as Apostles! I was still a little reluctant because I had a lot of friends in the ministry who like David said, "For it was not an enemy that reproached me; then I could have borne it: neither was it he that hated me that did magnify himself against me; then I would have hid myself from him: But it was thou, a man mine equal, my guide, and mine acquaintance" (Psalms 55:12). We took sweet counsel together, and walked unto the house of God in company, but it was a lot of "friends" sisters and brothers in Christ that I went to church with and served and sowed into building their ministries over the years that wounded my spirit that fell upon me. And it looked like they were right to the point I wondered if I had really heard God which further tormented my mind. All of this happened at the birthing of Fully Persuaded Ministries. To top it off the enemy used Human Resources at my beautiful job to nail the hammer in my mind to be discussed in my next book release, ***Out of Egypt: The Transference of Wealth!*** Watch for the release!

After months of battling depression, anxiety, fear, and stress in what I called my time and season of spiritual rehabilitation, I was in a place that seemed like and felt like I was having a spiritual abortion. I wish I could truly articulate how I felt like a vegetable and would have been committed to a life of demonic torment if I had taken the antidepressant medications my therapist strongly recommended because of the state of depression I was in. I asked her if she understood spiritual warfare and she said no. I told her that I was a Minister of the Gospel and I believe God will heal me. Whenever I talked to my son and visited him, talked to my grandkids, or business communications with colleagues and friends, it took everything in me to not fall apart. For two weeks I laid on the prayer line as the midwife in Dr. Cassandra Scott began to prophesy and speak life into my seemingly death situation. She kept saying, "You shall live and not die. God is not through with you yet. You don't think you're coming out of this attack but in the name of Jesus I command you to rise up and walk! Your voice is waiting to be heard and you are an Apostle to the nations. Get up woman of God. You thought you were going to die but today God is taking off your grave clothes like Lazarus. The devil never should have touched you.

It's not over!" Barely able to breathe, I cried even the more because I felt paralyzed but she kept breathing life into me. God began to say that it was all right to come out now and that Pastor C was someone I could trust and that she was covering me.

After God had spoken, I began to strengthen and to encourage myself in the Lord. It was time to come out of hiding and to walk on water and know the power of His Resurrection. I wanted to meet THE VOICE that was speaking and breathing life into me over a prayer line. Pastor C kept saying, *"You have a voice that the nations are waiting to hear. You shall decree a thing and it shall be established and the favor and the light shall shine upon your ways (Job 22:28) God knows what you've been through but this is your Turning Point!"*

Dorothy invited me to Pastor Scott's church one Friday night at the completion of a 40-day shift of prayer. The service was about to end and Pastor Scott was giving her closing remarks before the benediction. Earlier that day after the prayer line had ended, I had shared with Dorothy that I asked God to show me exactly who these women were on this prayer line because I do not want to get close to anybody anymore but I do want to meet Pastor Scott because her prayers and Prophetic declarations were healing my mind and healing my heart. God confirmed again that I could trust her and validated the authenticity of the anointing that was on her and gave me a full Prophetic revelation of the purpose and the power an army of intercessors He was gathering to shake nations for the Kingdom!

> PROPHETIC PRONOUNCEMENT: GOD WILL CONFIRM DIVINE KINGDOM KIN-NECTIONS AND YOUR GIFT WILL MAKE ROOM FOR YOU AND BRING YOU BEFORE GREAT MEN

I wrote it all down and brought it with me just in case an entrance was given to release the Prophetic word of the Lord. So I came but still I was not going to speak again because of the fear of what happened the last time I opened my mouth and preached and prayed and prophesied. But before Pastor Scott could close the service, Dorothy ran up on the platform, grabbed the mike, and called me out saying "Pastor C, my friend, Apostle Deborah, is here and she is carrying a revelation of the prayer line that God gave her this morning and you gotta hear it before we go." I thought I was off the hook and wanted to say "no, that's okay, another time." But God stood me up and Pastor C said, "Come on up here woman of God." The revelation shook the foundation! After nine months, the Lord gave me the Issachar anointing to understand the times and seasons and birthed out of me "Release the Sound," an Apostolic and Prophetic conference call to the nations every Thursday at 8:30p.m. We established the 12 Tribes of Israel on the prayer line and I accepted her invitation to be a Director leading the Tribe of Issachar!

The Spirit of False Accusations, Deception and all sorts of demonic spirits came against us but we kept moving forward. It has been three years that we have been on the prayer line of what has been affectionately called "a lifeline" and that's what it has literally been for countless men, women and children across the nation. For me, it has been the place God had prepared place for me to be raised from the dead and live to tell you the story! Remember the seed of the word of God is what produces life in you and therefore you must always remain in a place where that life can flow. You have to be connected to a life source ministry empowering kingdom connection that is not only going to equip and train you but to COVER AND PROTECT YOU while God totally and completely restores you! In the seasons and cycles of your life when you are ovulating, proper covering and divine spiritual alignment has a name given by God that will speak to your destiny as a THE VOICE of a midwife. Pastor Scott's ministry is named: Created2Produce! The names of the emerging new wineskins are not just nice names, they are called according to their purpose. Why seek ye the living amongst the dead? Many old structures are fading away and try as hard as you would like but some of the old structures simply must give way to the new. Get into a ministry that is going to build you up not tear you down – That's Apostolic and that was a prophetic revelation! Catch the Revelation and get connected to the true vine.

I DECREE AND DECLARE YOU SHALL NOT DIE BUT LIVE TO DECLARE THE GLORY OF THE LORD!
Then comes the end, when he shall have delivered up the kingdom to God, even the Father; when he shall have put down all rule and all authority and power.
For he must reign, till he has put all enemies under his feet.
The last enemy that shall be destroyed is death.
I Corinthians 1524-26

FRIENDS IN THE PROPHETIC PROCESS OF TIME

Through the prayer line I met an awesome Kingdom Kinnection whose voice always lifts my spirit and stirs up the gift in me to speak forth. Dr. Sabrina Echols is one of the Directors for the Tribe of Simeon who recently released a book entitled, "Voiceless" in which she describes too how the enemy wants to shut your mouth from sharing the gospel and being who God called you to be. The religious rulers, the heads of powers that rule over the kingdoms of the world systems are A-Okay until THE VOICE begins to speak to the nations. Dr. Echols speaks for those who are suffering mental and emotional sickness and fighting the disease of HIV/AIDS and travels to Africa to minister to hundreds of men, women, boys and girls.

The religious rulers and the Pharisees had no problem in the temple until THE VOICE, the Chief Apostle, Jesus Christ showed up and began turning over the tables. The Voice said, "My house shall be called a house of prayer and you have made it a den of thieves!" Jesus is turning over tables today and kicking out the money changers in the 21st Century movement as we SHIFT THE WEALTH OF NATIONS for righteousness and justice, fairness and equality tipping the scales of balance to bring order and correction back into the house – that's the apostolic, that's the Prophetic function – it is soooooo not a "title."

GOD'S ECONOMIC RECOVERY PLAN

PROPHETIC PRONOUNCEMENT: "FOR I KNOW THE PLANS I HAVE FOR YOU!"

Kay and Mark Miller are two of the most anointed ministry gifts in the Body of Christ who are raising up Apostolic and Prophetic Kingdom Life Coaches to "go ye into all the world and preach the Gospel of the Kingdom" and live the life God intended. The day after I was laid off my job Kay was like, "Deborah, this is perfect timing. You gotta come by the house – God has given me something that is going to knock your socks off and bless you to prosper!" Just what I needed since I just lost my only source of income. We met the following Tuesday and my socks were knocked off! What I discovered was my meeting Kay & Mark at that KAIROS moment in time was going to be more than an opportunity to create wealth, but the keys to the Kingdom that they shared through "A Course of A Lifetime" was the seed to activate the time clock to begin the transference of wealth for the restoration of the years that the locust and the palmerworm and the caterpillar have eaten out of our lives! This seed positioned me to believe God for the greatest financial, spiritual, economic, emotional and physical healing to complete His plan of renewing my mind, my heart, my spirit and my soul that was about totally transforming me for the rest of my life!

In the Prophetic process of time that is set for you to birth nations, you don't just need an intercessor, you need real true midwives, Apostolic Fathers and Spiritual Mothers who know how and when to snatch you out of the grip of the enemy who is ready to devour as soon as your child is born (Revelation 12:4). You are about to bring forth a nation's deliverance! The day I would finish writing this book Prophetess Dana called and woke me up out of a deep sleep around 7:45 am April 2nd. She asked me how was I doing and I just bust out crying! Telling her about the warfare and attacks coming against me and that I had not finished the book. My Executive Administrator, intercessor and friend, Pat Moses held my hand and wiped my forehead all that day even though physically she was at work, she stayed on the phone with me assuring me that I could do it. She went into the Holy Ghost and began to pray and prophesy like a real midwife will do when you are in labor and delivery! Be careful who you call or answer the phone to speak to you while you are in the labor and delivery room. Give no place to the devil – access is not granted to everybody but only to those assigned by God to PUSH you into your destiny.

TIME SENSITIVE

When the doctor pronounces that a woman is pregnant, there is a time sensitive date of nine months that is also given within which she must prepare to give birth. The closer she gets to the "due date" the closer the contractions come as the baby is repositioned to make its way through the birth canal. As you remain sensitive to the signs that what you are carrying is approaching the "due date" it is imperative that you be in position to lay hold of what God has promised.

In this 21st Century you must VALUE the time you set aside to be about your Father's business. Destiny wasters, dream killers are assigned to your every move to take your time, attention and focus from doing what God has called you to do. It will cost you the time you could have spent building the vision of that ministry, that business; planning and executing key personal financial moves you need to make in this season for the next season. I was sharing on my conference call a few months ago how it's winter but I'm already in the Spring time executing plans and making preparations for what I know God will have me to be doing in the Summer! Do you know what Season it is in your life? To everything there is a time and a season for every PURPOSE under the sun. Purpose dictates the season for a time to plant and a time to reap. Many are planting in a time they should be reaping a harvest. You cannot plant a garden in the Winter and expect a harvest in the Spring! The place of worship is the

Secret Place to receive the download of Prophetic revelation! CRUSH THE HEAD OF THE ENEMY by staying in position and finish the assignment!

DISMANTLING AND EVICTING DESTINY WASTERS

The game of distraction is won by the enemy when he takes your focus away to chase rabbits. Destiny wasters are disguised in the form of distractions whose objective is to take your attention and focus from God's will to meet someone else's desire. Distractions come in various forms but the objective is the same. The 21st Century guide for ministry in the 21st Century must include an increase in the gift the discerning of spirits. You must recognize the strategy of the enemy and shut it down! There is a limited amount of time to play games on Facebook when you are in the kairos timing of God carrying a set assignment to birth nations at a set time! In the birthing position, the transmission of the frequencies of Kingdom revelation are spiritual contractions you cannot allow anything or anyone to interrupt the time you need to hear God for your assignment. Your next move depends on receiving the download from Heaven in this season of your life.

Every time I logon to Facebook to check messages, there is someone (mostly those I accepted as "friends" who I don't know or ever engage in conversation with) who invites me to come play a game that I have never played, never heard of, and can't understand why do they think I want to play this game. These are thoughts that come to my mind as a mystery I care not to unlock! It's not arrogance; it just makes sense! I understand there are great games and apps out there on Facebook and other sites and in your cellphone. I love the benefits this social network offers. However, because I am always on assignment - trying to stay in God's timing to be in position to receive my spiritual inheritance to leave a legacy and fulfill my calling - I cannot play the game of distraction and neither can you.

Kick in the Issachar Factor, always being cognizant of the fact that this is a time to know what to do. Knowing this first, your adversary, the devil is like a roaring lion seeking whom he may devour – YOU – the one who is carrying the seed to birth nations. The enemy is not playing games on Facebook and is not following somebody else's Tweets! He is however, following your every move with "access granted" when you get distracted. The enemy uses technology and associated applications as devices to plan how he will hinder your progress by intentionally distracting and monitoring everything you say and do. You think it is a game? Think again. Unless you are playing with your children, participating in a recreational sport, you do not have time to play the game of distraction - not if you are called to the frontline for ministry to birth nations! The enemy also defeats many by having them in a state of slumber and slothfulness in conducting business and financial affairs. WAKE UP! Be sober, be vigilant because your adversary, the devil, is as a roaring lion seeking whom he may devour (I Peter 5:8, KJV)!

So I thank God for friends in the Prophetic process who push me into purpose! This is a poem I wrote that I read on the prayer line one day about that. It inspired so many to call me asking for a copy (here ya go!) I felt it would speak to this time and season of your life to help you understand the divine kin-nections that God is causing to help you through your birth pangs so that you can birth a nation and let go of the destiny wasters because it's time for you to bring forth!

FRIENDS IN THE PROPHETIC PROCESS OF PURPOSE

As we walk in the Prophetic process of purpose toward perfected destiny,
Many people will walk in and out of your life,
But only true friends, sons and daughters
Will leave footprints in your heart!
The people that walk out of your life
And leave scars there were never ordained to be
True friends for life - their season is over;
The summer has ended and the harvest is past.
Bless them for the part they played
But you must let them go!
Walk Into Your Season!
LIFE MAY NOT BE THE PARTY WE HOPED FOR, BUT WHILE WE'RE HERE WE SHOULD DANCE!

Chapter 16:

THE POWER OF HIS RESURRECTION

How God anointed Jesus of Nazareth with the Holy Ghost and with power: who went about doing good, and healing all that were oppressed of the devil; for God was with him
Acts 10:38

APOSTOLIC WARFARE IS WON IN WORSHIP

KEEP THE MUSIC PLAYING AND YOU WILL BE SHIFTING THE ATMOSPHERE!

The revelation of the Gospel of the Kingdom levels the playing field of religious exercise and ushers you into a level of warfare that you will have to experience and win for the anointing to birth nations. You will learn to fight the good fight of faith when the time comes to walk out the calling of God, you will soon discover this is not for the faint of heart. Ministry will make you or break you because of the level of the anointing that God has fitted you to carry out by the abundance of REVELATION that God is pouring out in these times of reformation in the 21st Century. Because this book is intended to speak to the nations the truth of Apostolic and Prophetic ministry, the strategies for successful spiritual warfare must be discussed. There is no way to avoid the confrontations of hostile enemies that are set against your mind as you carry out the assignment and perfect will of God. You cannot avoid it because the enemy cannot avoid you! You are such a force to be reckoned with that when you wake up in the morning, the powers of hell wake up trembling because for you to live is a daily fight it is a daily fight for the enemy to keep you down and out of position. It is often said that "the devil is busy" and the devil is busy because God is busy using you to birth nations. The assignment has not changed since Christ came the first time: To destroy the works of the devil. If I knew there was a group of people trying to destroy me, I would be busy too trying to stop them. I believe that many times we underestimate the power and authority we have been given by God to defeat Satan that we place his arsenal and warfare against us higher than the victory that Christ declares we already have against the battles we fight. If you are like me you should get tired of hearing "Christians" talking about how "busy the devil" is and want to scream, "So what are you going to do about it?" And God said tell them TO WORSHIP TO THE 7TH LEVEL FOR POWER! Apostolic warfare is won through your worship. You are seated in heavenly places, far above principalities and powers.

No matter what level of warfare that came against my purpose, God always gave me a song to carry me through my seasons. I recognized this and began years ago to keep a journal of the sound of worship that ministered to my spirit and kept me in the presence of God. Psalms 27:5: *"For in the time of trouble He shall hide me, in the secret of his tabernacle shall He hide me. He shall set me upon a rock"* has always been my meditation. "I Choose to Worship" by Wess Morgan became one of my favorite songs of worship that the Lord that God used to hide me under the shadow of the Almighty.

THROUGH THE FIRE

The true test of apostolic strength is realized when you go into the fire, the fourth man stands up, and you come out! Many have died in the fire, but you didn't. This should prove to you that you have been able to withstand seven times the heat that others did not survive. Have you ever wondered why you survived and others didn't? If you are reading this you should know like I know beyond any shadow of doubt that God has kept you alive on purpose and for His glory! The fact that I am writing this book is a testimony to you. When the enemy turned up the heat in my life, I was almost on the edge of losing my mind.

I remember years ago when I was on my patio preparing a fire to barbecue dinner for my son and me. Now if you want to know how to start a fire, I'm an expert so pay attention! LOL! My father (may he rest in peace) taught me to lay the charcoals in the barbecue pit, dowse it with lighter fluid, let it sit for a while to soak, and then light it. If you don't let it soak into the charcoals the fire would burn out. So while I followed his instructions and let it sit for a long time, I came out onto my patio, leaned over the charcoal and lit the fire. When I lit the charcoals, a blue fire jumped up into my face before I could move away. Feeling the moistness and heat upon my face and smelling the singe of burning hair, I ran screaming into the bathroom to look into the mirror expecting to see burns and blisters from the fire I literally felt on my face. I looked and to my amazement and utter surprise the fire did not touch me! This is one of those miracle moments when you hear like I heard the voice of the Lord saying,

But now thus says the LORD that created you, O Jacob, and he that formed you, O Israel, Fear not: for I have redeemed you, I have called you by your name; you are mine.
When you pass through the waters, I will be with you; and through the rivers,
they shall not overflow you:
WHEN YOU WALK THROUGH THE FIRE, YOU SHALL NOT BE BURNED;
neither shall the flame scorch you"
Isaiah 43:1-2, KJV

I believe that because the enemy has turned the heat up against the nations the Lord has given us a key to understanding the intensity of the heat of battle illustrated in the lives of three Hebrew boys who were thrown into the fire to bring us to a place of a deeper level of worship. When the enemy turns up the heat in your life, turn up the heat of your worship. Keep the music playing, turn up the volume, increase the frequency of time you enter into the Secret Place -

Worship in Warfare! It will change your form and appearance in the face of the enemy and the fourth man will stand up!

Then was Nebuchadnezzar full of fury, and the form of his appearance was changed against Shadrach, Meshach, and Abednego: therefore he spoke, and commanded that they should heat the furnace seven times more than it was usually heated.
Daniel 3:19

Did not we cast three men bound into the midst of the fire? They answered and said unto the king, True, O king. 25He answered and said, Lo, I see four men loose, walking in the midst of the fire, and they have no hurt; and the form of the fourth is like the Son of God
Daniel 3:24-25

THERE IS A RHYTHM TO HEAVEN WHEN WE WORSHIP!

Apostles have a keen ear to hear God because as do the Prophets, they worship well! To hear God is to worship Him in the beauty of His holiness. Theirs is a heart that beats with the sound of God that makes the whole body play a beautiful melody and function according to their gift to release the anointing. Because you are a worshipper you will know the voice of God and you will know the sound of God. That's why Jesus said often, "My sheep know my Voice" and a stranger they will not follow." The sound of the apostolic ministry is at a frequency that can only penetrate a heart that has been broken and mended to bring forth God's plans. This sound is at a pitch, tone and frequency that not everyone will hear even as it shall be in the last days when the last trumpet of God will sound.

When I look back over my life I can see how God anointed Jesus Christ of Nazareth as an example to show us how we are anointed by God through suffering. Retrospectively, I can see how God anointed my head with oil and how He brought me back to life. It's how God raised the foundation in me to Release the Sound. It's how God raised me from the dead. It's how He renewed my mind. My best friend and childhood friend Elaine Donaldson told me as I shared how God renewed my mind that, "Deb, not only did He renew your mind, but He gave you a new mind!" That's exactly how I see it and what I feel right now. Every time I think about how GOD brought me out, I cannot help but to praise Him. After the defeat of Sisera and his 900 chariots of iron, the prophetess and judge, Deborah, sang a song (Judges 5) I, too have a new song to sing:

THE 21ST CENTURY SONG OF DEBORAH!

Every time I worship with Pastor Marvin Sapp's song, "So Glad I made it, I made it through" I cry and I bow down. I know how He carried me. I know how He delivered me when I launched the ministry and the devil was set to devour it as soon as it was born. I know how: God picked me up and hid me in the wilderness, a place I was not familiar with. How He healed me; who He used to help me to deliver what was in me to deliver a nation! When you face the darkest hours of your life, when the enemy comes in like a flood, the Spirit of the Lord, nobody else, will lift up a standard against it! The power of His resurrection will LIFT you up!

I am so grateful to my mother who taught all of her children to memorize the 23rd Psalms. That psalm would be a spiritual covering of confession over me as I learned how to walk through the valley of the shadow of death.

- I WAS NOT SUPPOSED TO MAKE IT THROUGH THE VALLEY WHILE I SAW THE SHADOWS OF THE DEATH WALK AROUND MY MIND!
- I WAS SUPPOSED TO BE DEAD!
- MY VOICE WAS NEVER SUPPOSED TO BE HEARD AGAIN IN THE LAND!
- I WAS NOT SUPPOSED TO EVER BE ABLE TO THINK, TO WRITE, OR TO SPEAK!
- I WAS NEVER SUPPOSED TO BE ABLE TO WRITE LIKE A SCHOLAR!
- I WAS SUPPOSED TO LOSE MY MIND!

But the Spirit of the Lord LIFTED UP A STANDARD! The enemy can only go so far. My mother's choir used to sing a song, *"Whenever the Lord says Peace, There Will Be Peace."* Keep the music playing. Now I know that ALL THINGS work together for good, to them that love God and are called according to His purpose. Now I know that the power of God rests on me that I may know Him, the fellowship of His suffering and the Power of His Resurrection! I praise God that I am FULLY PERSUADED! Now I know that no weapon formed against me shall prosper and every tongue that has risen against me shall be condemned, especially after this book is released! This is the inheritance of the saints of God and it is the inheritance that is my bloodline, in my family, and – it is in yours too! You carry the seed – Oh the Blood of Jesus that washes white as snow! Surely goodness and mercy shall follow me all the days of my life and I will dwell in the house of the Lord forever!

He restored my reticular activating system and said to me, "Let this mind be in you which was also in Christ Jesus. Be ye renewed in the "spirit" of your mind are the words the Holy Spirit began to speak to me. You have overcome by the blood of the Lamb and by the word of your testimony. The garden of your genesis was severely attacked by the enemy in the place of the mind that is seated "In heavenly places" and you are seated far above principalities and powers and rulers of the darkness of this world! That's the Office of an Apostle demonstrated by Jesus Christ who defeated death, hell and the grave and is NOW SEATED at the Right Hand of the Father!

I can now testify that the same power that raised Christ Jesus up from the dead shall also quicken this mortal body!

Leah conceived again to bear Issachar and Deborah conceived again to birth multiple ministries. The seed in this woman has crushed the enemy's head!

The inhabitants of the villages ceased, they ceased in Israel,
UNTIL THAT I DEBORAH AROSE, THAT I AROSE A MOTHER IN ISRAEL.
They chose new gods; then was war in the gates:
was there a shield or spear seen among forty thousand in Israel?
Judges 5:7-8

CONCLUSION

As you begin to apply the revelation of this 21st Century Guide for 21st Century ministry, the true image of Christ, His Church (the Ekklesia), will be the process of transformation that begins a rebirth to discovering truth and unveiling of hidden mysteries to birth nations. When you are chosen to bring forth a Son to birth nations, it cannot be emphasized enough, the level of warfare that comes to attack your mind. The enemy's purpose was that I would lose my mind so that I would never be able to think, write, articulate the mind of Christ and speak as an oracle of God. It is with the mind that we serve the Lord. The devil loves to play "mind games" so that you will be taken away from the main purpose: TO CRUSH THE HEAD OF THE ENEMY.

It is my prayer that you will understand your true identity and begin to see the nations that you are called to birth into the truth and light of God's word. You are not members in an institutionalized framework of a physical building, but you are Ambassadors for Christ, a Royal Priesthood and a Holy Nation! The closing song of my season I leave with you,

"The Blessing of Abraham" by Donald Lawrence:

> *"Kingdom people God's got you so covered you*
> *just go on and build Kingdoms.*
> *The Blessing Is On You*

I am the God that healeth thee
Wherever you, whatever you touch
It's Anointed to Grow
YOU ARE THE SEED! By faith receive
THE BLESSING OF ABRAHAM!"

Humbly Submitted,
Apostle Deborah L. Anderson
Ambassador and Speaker of the House

IT IS FINISHED!

FULLY PERSUADED
Ministries

REFERENCES

The Holy Bible, King James Version

The Holy Bible, Amplified

The Holy Bible, The Message Version

GOD'S WORD® Translation (©1995)

Easton's Bible Dictionary M.G. Easton M.A., D.D., Illustrated Bible Dictionary, Third Edition, published by Thomas Nelson, 1897

Wikipedia, The Free Encyclopedia on Post Christianity Internet: http://en.wikipedia.org/wiki/Postchristianity#cite_note-0. Retrieved March 19, 2013

Wikipedia, The Free Encyclopedia on Systematic Theology Internet: http://en.wikipedia.org/wiki/Systematic_theology Retrieved March 19, 2013

Wikipedia, The Free Encyclopedia on Hermeneutics Internet: http://en.wikipedia.org/wiki/Hermeneutics Retrieved: April 8, 2013

Viljoen, Dave, "Rediscovering Authentic Christianity, An Apostolic Reformation" (2010)

Eckhardt, John, "The Ministry Anointing of The Apostle"

The Word Network Quote by Will Smith Internet: http://www.facebook.com/thewordnetwork. Retrieved March 19, 2013

The Pew Forum on Religion and Public Life, The Stronger Sex - Spiritually Speaking. Internet: http://www.pewforum.org/The-Stronger-Sex----Spiritually-Speaking.aspx Retrieved May 18, 2013

The Pew Forum on Religion and Public Life, Religion Among the Millennials (POLL February 17, 2010): Less Religiously Active Than Older Americans, But Fairly Traditional In Other Ways. Internet: http://www.pewforum.org/Age/Religion-Among-the-Millennials.aspx. Retrieved May 18, 2013

Harvey, Steve, "Act Like a Lady, Think Like A Man," Harper Collins Publishers. Internet: http://www.harpercollins.com/book/index.aspx?isbn=9780061728976. Retrieved: May 31, 2013

The National Law Forum on Recent Cases, eDiscovery & Social Media, Internet: http://nationallawforum.com/2010/11/29/ediscovery-social-media. Retrieved: April 3, 2013, 2013

Better Health Channel
Internet:
http://www.betterhealth.vic.gov.au/bhcv2/bhcarticles.nsf/pages/Twins_identical_and_fraternal. Retrieved March 20, 2013

Eby, J. Preston, Kingdom Bible Studies
Internet: http://sigler.org/eby/REV26.htm. Retrieved March 22, 2013

R. David Rightmire, Dictionaries - Baker's Evangelical Dictionary of Biblical Theology , "Apostle" Internet: http://www.biblestudytools.com/dictionary/apostle/ Retrieved: March 23, 2013

Munroe, Dr. Myles, "Your gift will make room for you" by Dr. Myles Munroe, by Turning Point Zone (Notes) on Wednesday, January 13, 2010 at 9:19am; Internet: Facebook:http://www.facebook.com/notes/turning-point-zone/your-gift-will-make-room-for-you-by-dr-myles-munroe/249108294450; Retrieved: March 23, 2013

Pierce, Chuck, "A Time To Advance" (2011)

Echols, Dr. Sabrina S., "Voiceless" (2013)

The Hidden Evil. Internet:
http://www.thehiddenevil.com/psychopathy.asp Retrieved: March 26, 2013

The Mask of Sanity, Milton, Dr. Hervey. (1903 - January 28, 1984)

Hare, Dr. Robert, "Without Conscience" (January 8, 1999)

Wikipedia, Prima Facie
Internet: http://en.wikipedia.org/wiki/Prima_facie
Retrieved: March 26, 2013

Innovation and Information for Sustainable Living, "What is the function of Reticular Activating System? Internet: http://www.innovateus.net/health/what-function-reticular-activating-system. Retrieved: March 26, 2013

Trimm, Dr. Cindy, Quote: "If your context is wrong, then your conclusion will be wrong."

Jakes, Bishop T.D., "God's Leading Ladies"

FULLY PERSUADED
Ministries

Songs of my Seasons

2009-2012

Credits to all of the Gospel Recording Artists of the 21st Century who worshipped me through my seasons of adversity and gave me my identity back

I'll Trust You	James Fortune and FIYA
So Glad I Made It	Marvin Sapp
Draw Me Close	Marvin Sapp
Never Would Have Made It	Marvin Sapp
The Battle Is Not Yours	Yolanda Adams
I Choose To Worship	Wess Morgan
Faithful Is Our God	Hezekiah Walker
Moving Forward	Hezekiah Walker
It's A New Season	Israel Houghton
As We Worship	Wess Morgan
Release the Rivers of God	Shekinah Glory
No Limits No Boundaries	Israel Houghton & New Breed
There Is A King In You	Donald Lawrence
Walk Into Your Season	Donald Lawrence
The Law of Confessions	Donald Lawrence
The Blessing Is On You	Donald Lawrence
The Blessing of Abraham	Donald Lawrence

Special Credits and Thanks

To contributing editors, intercessors and midwives who helped me to push while in labor and delivery completing this book

Prophetess Rosemary Washington
Minister Nicolette Hines
Minister Cynthia Patterson
Patricia Moses
Prophetess Dana Carmouche
Elaine Donaldson
Sheryl Norton
Tanika Guidroz

HIGHLY RECOMMENDED READING

A Course of A Lifetime By Kay Miller

Meeting the Ethical Challenges of Leadership – 2nd Edition by Craig E. Johnson

Joyce & Jason in the Adventures of Genesis by Tanika Guidroz

Paul & His Prison Letters by John B. Pohill

About The Author

Apostle Deborah L. Anderson

A frontline warrior in the army of the Lord! Her ministry carries an Apostolic and Prophetic anointing as a Trumpet of God, called to shake nations and subdue kingdoms. A highly sought after speaker, mentor, and spiritual mother to many sons and daughters, she has ministered in conferences and business organizations for over 23 years. Her stature in the spirit carries great influence and impacts people with her unique presentation of the Gospel enabling her to minister to people in every walk of life.

A native of South Bend, Indiana, Deborah is a graduate of George Washington H.S., and received an Associate Business degree from Michiana College of Commerce, a Bachelor of Science Degree in Theology from Calvary Temple Seminary and Emmanuel Temple School of the Bible, with honors. She also earned a Paralegal Certification from Southwestern Professional Institute, State Bar accredited. Deborah received a Bachelor of Business Administration Degree at LeTourneau University in Houston, Texas graduating Summa Cum Laude - highest honor, highest praise. With a Governmental Anointing, she is in pursuit of obtaining a Juris Doctorate degree to become a Corporate, Civil Rights, Criminal Law and Family attorney with a prophetic voice to speak to nations advocating for civil justice and fairness. She will retire as a Righteous Judge-Prophetess as "Deborah" in the Book of Judges leading nations to victory. She is also a member of the Christian Legal Society, a national organization of lawyers and judges who inspire, encourage, and equip Christian lawyers and law students to proclaim, love and serve Jesus Christ through the study and practice of law, provision of legal assistance to the poor and needy, and the defense of the inalienable rights to life and religious freedom A creative, compassionate, business savvy, inspirational speaker, Deborah is a voice for the 21st Century whose time has come to be heard! She is the proud mother of a very gifted and anointed son, Rashon LaVelle Anderson and three grandchildren that are destined for greatness, Roman Gabriel, Brea Lois-Cyian, and Rashon LaVelle, Jr.

Made in the USA
Columbia, SC
07 August 2017